1790

Contents

The publishers wish to express their gratitude to the following who have given permission to use copyrighted illustrations in this book:

British Columbia Government, page 41.
British Columbia Hydro and Power Authority, page 37.
Canadian Government Travel Bureau, page 31.
Glenbow-Alberta Institute, pages 15, 16, 47.
Hudson's Bay Company, pages 6, 33.
Information Canada, page 8.
Information Canada Photothèque, page 28.
McCord Museum, Montreal, page 48.
The National Gallery of Canada, title page and page 3.
Public Archives of Canada, pages 18, 50, 52, 57.
J. K. Smith, page 24.
United States National Park Service, page 13.
Vancouver Centennial Museum, page 23.
The portrait of Lord Selkirk on page 58 is from the painting ascribed to Raeburn at St. Mary's Isle, Scotland, reproduced in *Canada and Its Provinces* (ed.) Adam Shortt (Reprinted. Toronto: University of Toronto Press, 1967).

Every effort has been made to credit all sources correctly. The author and publishers will welcome any information that will allow them to correct any errors or omissions.

The Author

James K. Smith has a special interest in the history of Canadian exploration and the fur trade.

To the "first man West"

© 1976 Fitzhenry & Whiteside Limited
    150 Lesmill Road
    Don Mills, Ontario, M3B 2T5

Written, printed and bound in Canada

ISBN-0-88902-225-9

The Legend of Alexander Mackenzie

Canadians have good reason to be proud of Alexander
Mackenzie. The trader-explorer who twice led a group of
men through the North American wilderness on extremely difficult, dangerous voyages of discovery is
honoured as the first man to reach the Pacific overland
north of Mexico. His transcontinental crossing predates
the American Lewis and Clark expedition by twelve years
and is a Canadian "first." Even Bernard DeVoto, that
eminent, Utah-born historian of continental exploration,
says of Mackenzie, "In courage, in the faculty of command, in ability to meet the unforeseen with resources of
craft and skill, in the will that cannot be overborne, he
has had no superior in the history of American exploration." Mackenzie must also be given credit for another
admirable accomplishment: in the course of these
journeys, he neither harmed an Indian nor lost a man.

Like many of history's heroes, Mackenzie had a great
deal of charm. A handsome, dark-eyed Highlander, he
had a stubborn mouth and chin that must have caused
many a woman's heart to flutter. An elegant dresser and
an easy conversationalist, he became a much sought after
member of Montreal and, later, London society. He was
the delight of every notable hostess and the despair of
mothers with marriageable daughters because he adored
supper parties, private dances, public balls – and every
pretty girl. (He managed to avoid matrimony until he was
48 years old.) In male gatherings, he was a cheerful
drinking companion, doubtless adding much laughter to
the conversation with his dry, often droll remarks. His
book, *Voyages from Montreal*, was a bestseller, and its
various English, American, French, German, and Russian
editions gave vicarious excitement to thousands upon
thousands of readers.

As a trader-explorer, Mackenzie fully appreciated the value of good relationships. He always treated his Indian customers firmly but fairly. He habitually used a blend of fatherly sternness and kindness when dealing with his voyageurs, which is the basic reason these canoemen served him so loyally and so magnificently. And, in the course of his explorations, he often walked casually into a village full of agitated, suspicious Indians and calmed them down by giving their children gifts of sugar and trinkets.

Mackenzie also had one outstanding characteristic that explains his early success in life: a bulldog-like determination to succeed in any enterprise he attempted, whatever the personal cost or risk — and regardless of anyone's opposition.

All these are facts. They add up to a legendary tale that is faithfully retold in book after book about him. Indeed, Mackenzie's numerous biographers have devoted the bulk of their attention to his explorations. It is for these incredible journeys that he will always be remembered. Yet these journeys are only the story of two summers in the life of a man who spent 33 years in the fur trade. Mackenzie was, by turns, a salesman, a sales manager, and then an executive whose daily work brought him in contact with other fur-trade executives and also with government officials in Canada, the United States, and Great Britain. The strange thing about Mackenzie's career — revealed in his *Voyages from Montreal* but ignored by almost everyone who has written about Mackenzie — is that he was much more than a daring explorer. He was a hard-headed businessman and a political visionary. His explorations were only two episodes in a career largely devoted to reorganizing and unifying the Canadian fur trade. Surprisingly, in the process of trying to bring about his reorganization and unification, Mackenzie almost qualifies as a very early father, perhaps a grandfather, of the federation of provinces called Canada.

Another very strange thing about Mackenzie's career is that he did not achieve the really important goals he set himself. True, he found a way to the Pacific Ocean, which he succeeded in doing before he was 30 years old. But what happened to him during the rest of his life is a very peculiar story of unconquered difficulties and a series of personal frustrations. In fact, a time came when Mackenzie's own business colleagues would have nothing to do with him and barred him from any day-to-day management in fur-trade matters. And the last years of Mackenzie's working life pose several puzzling questions that are difficult to answer satisfactorily. Why was he unable to unify into one great company all the firms working in the Canadian fur trade? Why was he unable to persuade the British government to contest the steady, westward movement of the American people and claim ownership of large territories in western North America? Why, within one year of his death, did other men achieve goals Alexander Mackenzie sought for most of his life?

This is the only known likeness of Alexander Mackenzie, who was about 35 or 36 years old when this portrait was painted. The artist, Thomas Lawrence, is said to have produced sparkling, life-like portraiture rather than the idealized paintings favoured by so many of his contemporaries.

Chapter 1 **An Emigrant Lad**

Cut off, in the cold, grey water of the Atlantic, from the extreme, northeast coast of Scotland is a long straggling line of islands called the Outer Hebrides. On the largest of these, Lewis, is the tiny fishing port and Hebridean capital of Stornoway. Here, in 1764, Alexander Mackenzie was born.

Natives of the Hebrides have long earned a living by cultivating stony soils and fishing the wild waters of the Atlantic. The Mackenzie family, however, seems to have been moderately well off, owning both a farm two miles from Stornoway and a house — in which Alexander was born — in the town itself. There were four children: Murdoch, who went to sea at an early age and was drowned, Alexander, Sybilla, and Margaret.

Almost nothing is known of Alexander's childhood. He himself never refers to it. Other sources offer mere scraps of information about an adventurous lad who loved to swim, fish, and lead other boys into mischief. There are, nonetheless, two distinct versions of how Alexander emigrated to North America. One of these says that he did not get on very well with his stepmother and left home of his own accord at the age of 15, shipping out from Glasgow as a deckhand on a vessel bound for Montreal. This account has a very romantic ring to it, but the testimony of some of Mackenzie's descendants suggests a quite different story.

It seems his mother died when he was ten years old, and he was taken by his father to New York City to stay with his paternal uncle, a very successful, very rich merchant. The boy had barely settled down in his new home when the American War of Independence (1775-1783) broke out. His father and uncle immediately obtained commissions as officers in a Loyalist regiment. The father died near Kingston (Ontario) a few years later, apparently from an attack of scurvy. Meanwhile, Alexander was being cared for by two aunts. Concerned for

his safety, they took him to upper New York State.
Sometime later, as the war spread into the wilderness of
the state's interior, they sent him to live with friends in
Montreal.

The first reliable information about Alexander's career
is that, in 1779, at the age of 15, he began to earn his
living. He became a clerk in the counting-house of Finlay,
Gregory & Company, a firm of Montreal fur merchants.
In the Preface to his *Voyages from Montreal*, he tells us
why he chose this particular occupation:

> I was led, at an early period of life, by commercial views, to the
> country northwest of Lake Superior in North America, and being
> endowed by nature with an inquisitive mind and enterprising
> spirit, possessing also a constitution and frame of body equal to
> the most arduous undertakings, and being familiar with toilsome
> exertions in the prosecution of mercantile pursuits . . .

In a roundabout fashion and in rather lofty prose,
Mackenzie admits to seeking his fortune. And this could
be done in the fur trade — provided you were healthy,
hardy, and hardworking. You also had to be lucky: the
history of the trade includes not a few incidents when a
man drowned, starved, or froze to death.

For some reason or other, the five years that Alexander
spent keeping account books for Finlay & Gregory are a
complete blank. The *Voyages* and his correspondence
ignore this period, and there is no other known record of
these youthful years. Oddly enough, Alexander Mackenzie makes almost as sudden an appearance in history
as he does in the *Voyages* — the skilful, successful fur
trader and dauntless, determined explorer whose dis-
coveries amazed and excited his day and age. Perhaps any
diaries kept during these years were lost in the fire that
destroyed his home in Scotland some years after his
death. Since Mackenzie was a very proud, very sensitive
individual, he may have destroyed papers and letters
belonging to a period of time when he was a complete
unknown. The obscurity of his early years could also be
explained by the need to learn his occupation. Hard work,
painstaking study, and attention to every last tiny detail
were marked characteristics of Alexander Mackenzie. So
he may well have devoted these years in Montreal to
acquiring a thorough grasp of the history, geography,
and economics of an activity that was as old as the first
arrival of Europeans in the Gulf of St. Lawrence.

Doubtless the youngster derived his knowledge of the fur trade from several sources, but he probably received a great deal of it from his senior employer, James Finlay. A Scot who came to Montreal soon after the collapse of the French régime, Finlay had been one of the first British traders — perhaps the very first — to venture 2,000 miles north and west of Montreal and reach that great highway of the prairies, the Saskatchewan River. The fact that he was in territory long considered the legal property of the Hudson's Bay Company (HBC) didn't worry Finlay for one moment. When one or two Company men he met accused him of trespassing and ordered him out of their employer's lands, Finlay's reply was to offer each of them employment with him at £25 per year (a much larger salary than the HBC was paying them), plus paid passage to Montreal. Finlay was equally confident in dealings with his customers. He built his trading post deep in Indian country, not far from where the Saskatchewan is formed by the junction of its great northern and southern branches. And those Indians who preferred to canoe on down to Hudson Bay and trade their fur pelts there found some of Finlay's voyageurs waiting for them at two different places downriver with canoe-loads of trinkets, muskets, powder, shot, tobacco — and rum. The lesson of Finlay's experiences would not be lost on Alexander: in order to succeed in trade, you had to be an aggressive salesman.

This scene, by an unknown artist, is described as the first sale of furs at Garraway's Coffee House, London, England, in 1671. Where had those furs come from? Who had obtained them?

Something else that must really have impressed the boy clerk was the enormous amounts of money that could be made. With the aid of twelve voyageurs, in his first winter on the Saskatchewan, Finlay cleared a profit of almost £3,000. He used this money to establish his own company in Montreal. Successive winters on the Saskatchewan enabled him to build up a very prosperous operation and enter into partnership with John Gregory, a young English merchant with excellent business connections in London, England. As Alexander saw on the pages of Finlay, Gregory's ledgers every day of the working week, his employers imported goods from Britain at very low prices and sold most of them to Indians at very high ones. Profits were usually at least 100 per cent. Incredibly, the whole business was the result of a persistent fashion in men's hats. From the late sixteenth century until well into the nineteenth century, the beaver hat was a status symbol in Europe.

While Alexander was earning his daily bread in a dingy, dusty office next door to a warehouse that was occasionally filled to the rafters with vile-smelling furs, several of his elders in Montreal were making money hand over fist. For many years, all the action was along the Saskatchewan River. During the bitter, bloody campaigns of the Seven Years' War (1756-1763), the French had been unable to spare men, money, and materials to maintain trade at their western fur posts. Thus there was an extremely profitable market waiting to be exploited when the war ended. Wealthy Europeans had been cut off from a major source of supply of the beaver pelts from which their fashionable hats were made. At the same time, the Indians of the upper Great Lakes region and the Saskatchewan River country had been deprived of the manufactures (axes, chisels, knives, muskets, combs, mirrors, shawls, thread, needles) that their own cultures had never produced and to which they had become accustomed — almost addicted — by many years of commerce with the French. Indians hungered particularly for firearms and ammunition and for the free liquor that preceded or accompanied every trading session. And the Montreal fur merchants who sent trader-employees hundreds of miles west to the Saskatchewan country discovered that they were only competing among themselves for furs. The Hudson's Bay Company, comfortable

It was not uncommon to sell an item to an Indian trapper or his wife at 500 times the original costs of manufacture in Britain and transportation to North America.

Various types of beaver hats. What were the two main reasons a beaver hat was considered the most desirable headgear a man could wear?

The D'Orsay
1820

The Paris Beau
1815

Navy cocked hat
1800

Beaver pelts hung up to dry in a fashion used for hundreds of years.

and complacent in its depots on Hudson and James Bays and accustomed to securing its western supplies of furs from Indians living well north of the Saskatchewan, continued its general policy of enticing these customers to trade at its saltwater posts at Churchill and York.

Then something happened to change the direction of the entire fur trade and, as one result, accelerate Alexander Mackenzie's rise to fame and fortune.

James Finlay was just one of many adventurers who bartered for furs in the forests and plains to the north and west of the Great Lakes. Some of these "Pedlars from Montreal," as HBC men called them, were from the American colonies. A few were French Canadian. However many of them came from Europe — in particular, from the Highlands of Scotland. Since the great demand in Europe for beaver hats showed no signs of decreasing, the tempo of competition quickened in the *pays d'en haut*, the name voyageurs gave to the forests and plains north of the Great Lakes. All the "Pedlars" became steadily greedier in their business dealings. Their only concern was to grab up pelts by the hundreds, if not by the thousands. It didn't matter how many Indians were cheated or robbed outright in the process. It was of no consequence whether a trader used liquor, cunning, or threats — or all three — provided that he could send canoeloads of pelts back east each summer to his sponsors. In fact, the Pedlars thrived on cutthroat competition and regularly engaged in price wars. And if a trader consistently outsold his immediate rivals, he was highly rated, even by those he had outsmarted.

Among these early adventurers in the pays d'en haut was a born wanderer from Connecticut called Peter Pond. He was a loner, and a quick-tempered one at that, although he always seemed to get on well with Indians. Pond, however, was basically a very confident, extremely aggressive man, one of a tough breed in a tough business.

Peter Pond was, by turns, soldier, sailor, shoemaker, fur trader, and explorer. But his most enduring contribution to history is that he pioneered the trade far beyond the Saskatchewan River and personally inspired Alexander Mackenzie to carry on the search after him. Not that Mackenzie ever admits that this was the case. In the *Voyages*, he gives Pond the barest credit for journeying into territories probably never seen before by Europeans,

and establishing a fur-trading operation that quickly
surpassed that of the Saskatchewan country in immediate
profit and future potential. In his book, Mackenzie
ignores, too, the fact that Pond also gathered much
valuable information from Indians, traders, and voyageurs on how the Pacific Ocean could be reached overland. Anything Mackenzie writes about the man who
was for a time his boss is quite brief, almost patronizing.

In all fairness to Mackenzie, Pond was a difficult man
to get along with. He had a reputation for violence: he
killed a fellow trader in rather vague, unexplained cir-
cumstances, and had a hand in the deaths of two others.
Nonetheless, whatever Pond's defects of character, his
exploratory work had a tremendous influence on Mackenzie's career. And the beginnings of this influence go
all the way back to the year before Alexander joined
Finlay & Gregory.

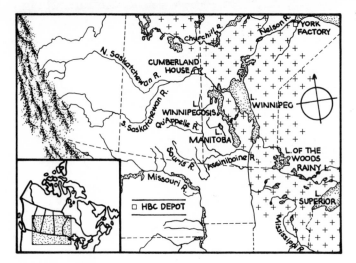

THE WESTERN INTERIOR

Chapter 2 The Young Trader

In the opening section of the *Voyages* entitled "A General History of the Fur Trade," Mackenzie writes,

... in the spring of the year 1778, some of the traders on the Saskatchewan River, finding that they had a quantity of goods to spare, agreed to put them into a joint stock, and gave the charge and management of them to Mr. Peter Pond, who, in four canoes, was directed to enter the English River [the Churchill River] .... and proceed still farther, if possible, to Athabasca, a country hitherto unknown but from Indian report. In this enterprise, he at length succeeded ...

Mackenzie's account of this pioneer expedition into the pays d'en haut ignores the harsh realities of Pond's epic journey. There were dozens of portages caused by the wildly plunging cascades and rapids of the Churchill; and its placid stretches of water often concealed masses of tree debris that were close enough to the surface to rip gaping holes in birchbark canoes. Once as far west on the Churchill as Lake Ile-à-la-Crosse (in northwestern Saskatchewan), Pond's search took him northward. He and his men had to haul canoes and cargoes over the 12-mile-long Methye Portage, the height of land that separates waters flowing to Hudson Bay from those flowing to the Arctic Ocean. Once across the punishing Methye Portage and embarked on the Clearwater, a tributary of the Athabasca River, Pond found himself in a landscape completely different from that along the Churchill or Saskatchewan Rivers. He had entered Athabasca — a subarctic region 3,000 miles from Montreal which, with its hundreds of lakes and thousands of square miles of muskeg, is more water than land. It has been aptly remarked of Athabasca that "the country is four-fifths drowned and when not frozen is half-hidden by mosquitoes and black flies." But he was looking at the richest fur region the trade would ever know.

Of all the merchants operating Montreal fur firms, only a handful grasped the long-term significance of Pond's discovery. On the one hand, he had had to travel farther into the pays d'en haut than any other trader, and this had cost his sponsors a great deal of money. But some

of Pond's Montreal acquaintances were utterly amazed by
the magnificently heavy, lustrous Athabasca pelts. Far to
the north and west where winters are eight, even nine,
months long, animal furs are correspondingly thick and
glossy. Each of these merchants was struck by the same
thought: with superb furs such as these, a man could
make a fortune several times over. The result was a prolonged effort by these particular men to make Athabasca
their exclusive sales territory. One of them was John
Gregory, the junior owner of Finlay & Gregory.

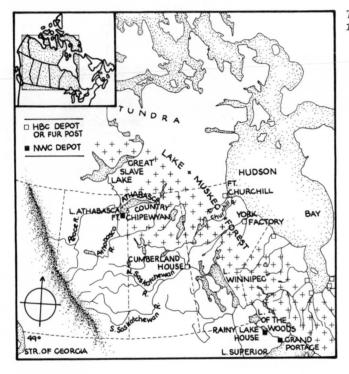

*THE CANADIAN WEST,
1785*

Five years after Pond's journey into Athabasca, James
Finlay retired and sold his interest in the company he
had founded. John Gregory immediately invited Norman
McLeod, an aggressive Detroit trader, to become his co-
owner. And Alexander Mackenzie suddenly found himself an active associate of these men, a promotion awarded
him as a result of a very successful trading mission he
undertook somewhere in the Detroit region in 1784.
Asked at short notice to leave his accounting duties and
take on the job of trader, he had proved to be a cool-

headed, competent salesman, able to hold his own against much older, more experienced men. In fact, Mackenzie did so well that he was offered a partnership in Gregory, McLeod on condition that he went to work in the pays d'en haut in 1785. A race was on to grab as many Athabasca furs as possible.

Mackenzie, of course, eagerly accepted the offer and its condition. He was given charge of the Churchill River region and established his headquarters at Lake Ile-à-la-Crosse. Alexander's nearest colleague, his cousin Roderick McKenzie, an apprentice trader, was at a post farther down the Churchill. Several hundred miles to the north and west in Athabasca, another colleague, John Ross, was up against Peter Pond, who was working for the only opposition of any note: the North West Company.

For the next year or two, the sales force of Gregory, McLeod must have offered their competitors a spirited opposition. Few details of this period in the trade or in Mackenzie's career have survived. All we have to go on are his own characteristically brief comments in the "General History" section of the *Voyages*:

> . . . after the severest struggle ever known . . . and suffering every oppression which a jealous and rival spirit could instigate; after the murder of one of our partners [in the winter of 1786/87], the laming of another, and the narrow escape of one of our clerks, who received a bullet through his powder horn in the execution of his duty, they [the North West Company] were compelled to allow us a share of the trade . . .

The murdered man was John Ross. It seems that Pond had encouraged his voyageurs to harass Ross and bully Indians into not offering him any furs. As a result, one voyageur, Péché by name, shot Ross when he was attempting to stop a group of Pond's men from forcibly taking some Chipewyan customers to their master's post to trade.

"High wine" was a concentrated mixture of wine and liquor whose bulk could be doubled, tripled, or even quadrupled by the later addition of water.

Even before the murder of Ross, competition between the North West Company and Gregory, McLeod had been vicious. Hundreds of gallons of liquor and of "high wine" had been smuggled out of Montreal in kegs that were labelled gunpowder, sugar or salt. In the pays d'en haut, these intoxicants were used to bribe or befuddle Indians into trading with one or other company. But the rivals employed too much liquor too often. So many customers maimed or killed relatives and other tribe members in the course of drinking sessions that word of this filtered back to officials in Quebec who were responsible for the regulation of the fur trade. Angered by the illegal use of liquor in what was, officially, Indian territory and, finally, shocked by the murder of one trader by another, British authorities in Quebec warned the two companies to act together or be denied the annual licences permitting them to engage in the trade.

So the rivals joined forces. In the summer of 1787, at the depot of Grand Portage on Lake Superior, the senior personnel of Gregory, McLeod — including Alexander Mackenzie, who happened to be at the depot that summer — were created partners in the North West Company.

The history of the North West Company, which probably began some time in the middle or late 1770s, is quite complex because its membership was often a changing, usually expanding one. The name alone is confusing because the organization itself was composed of a number of individual fur companies. However, the North West Company was never at any time in its existence a company in the normal sense of a legally constituted corporation accountable for its actions, financing, et cetera. It was simply a trading name used by a loose association of men who worked in the same line of business and agreed to turn it into a very profitable livelihood by creating what amounted to a monopoly. Certain well-financed Montreal fur merchants established copartnerships with each other and also with a number of "wintering partners," each firm's senior traders in the pays d'en haut — "Nor'Westers," as they proudly called themselves — and used the handy title of the North West Company to describe their common business activities.

From the beginning the Company was immensely successful. Nor'Westers displayed unrelenting opposition to anyone who was not of their number. They acted as if they *owned* the pays d'en haut. Whether competing with traders working for other Montreal companies or with men from the Bay, they often used Mafia-like tactics — threatening violence; hijacking their competitors' supplies of goods; and bribing, bullying, or intoxicating Indians into becoming their customers. Indeed many Nor'Westers in effect controlled groups of Indians by making them dependent upon handouts of liquor. If these tactics didn't

The restored "Great Hall" at Grand Portage, where North West Company executives met each summer to settle matters of salaries and profits, promotions and retirements, trade policies and expansion plans.

Grand Portage was a depot, so what other buildings would it contain?

work, their colleagues in Montreal sometimes neutralized competition by bringing rivals into the Company as fellow partners and giving them a share of the profits.

These colleagues also handled the Company's public relations. When making applications for annual licences to trade in the pays d'en haut, the Montreal members were always careful to give British officials in Quebec the impression that their wintering associates were an admirable group of trader-explorers who were busy extending the limits of British influence and territory in North America. They described themselves as merchants devoted to fostering the flow of furs and goods between Quebec and London. Ruthless, powerful, but outwardly respectable, the North West Company was one of the earliest examples of "Big Business" in North America.

In his "General History" Mackenzie gives an inside view of the Company's very simple but very successful financial structure, which had been cleverly organized to offer each member a strong incentive to work as hard as he could. Mackenzie's account explains exactly why the Nor'Westers were such fierce competitors:

> ... It [the Company] consisted [in 1787] of twenty shares, unequally divided among the persons concerned. Of these, a certain proportion was held by the people who managed the business in Canada, and were styled agents for the Company. Their duty was to import the necessary goods from England, store them at their own expense at Montreal, get them made up into the articles suited to the trade, pack and forward them, and supply the cash that might be wanting for the outfits [clerks' and voyageurs' wages, and the purchase of food supplies], for which they received, independent of the profit on their shares, a commission .... The remaining shares were held by the proprietors [traders] who were obliged to winter and manage the business of the concern with the Indians .... Some of them, from their long service and influence, held double shares and were allowed to retire from the business at any period ... with one of these shares, naming any young man in the Company's service to succeed him in the other [that is, by buying the share] .... Thus all the young men succeeded in succession to the character and advantages of partners .... This ... mode of providing for the clerks [apprentice traders] of the Company excited a spirit of emulation in the discharge of their various duties .... Indeed, without such a spirit, such a trade could not have become so extended and advantageous ....

In the period 1790-95, the annual Company profit averaged £72,000 and rose to £98,000 for each of the last four years of the century — at a time when an income of £1,500 to £2,000 a year was considered a comfortable living.

Clerks were paid a salary that varied with length of service and was anywhere from £100 to £400 annually, and they were also supplied with food and clothing. The partners received several hundred pounds apiece after the year's annual profit was calculated and then divided by the number of shares.

In the year in which he became a Nor'Wester, Alexander Mackenzie was ordered to winter in Athabasca with Peter Pond. The appointment as second-in-command of the Company's Athabasca Department was a considerable compliment, clear recognition of his brief but impressive record as a hard-headed, hard-working trader. He had been picked out by the management of the North West Company as a promising candidate for promotion to executive position. The experience of supervising the vast, fur-rich Athabasca country — and whatever fur territories lay beyond — would prepare him for even greater Nor'Wester responsibilities in future years.

"Carriers of the North" by John Innes. York boats transporting trade goods and supplies to an HBC post.

*"A Portage" also by John
Innes. Canots du nord and
contents being lugged
around a steep falls.*
   *Why did the men from
the Bay and the Montrealers
use such radically different
watercraft?*

As soon as he received instructions to winter in Athabasca, Mackenzie ordered his voyageurs to have cargo
and canoes ready for him as quickly as possible. His
destination was 2,000 miles away in the Northwest, and
he had to get there with men and supplies before ice on
the waters of the pays d'en haut made navigation
impossible.

When Mackenzie left the depot of Grand Portage and
climbed up the nine-mile "Grande Portage" trail to its
western end, he found his canoemen patiently waiting for
him. Dressed in working clothes of moccasins, deerskin
leggings, breechclouts, and loose shirts or deerhide
jerkins, and with their hair hanging down around their
shoulders to give them some protection against the
millions of insects that infested the north country, they
looked like a band of desperadoes. The men squatted or
lolled on the ground beside the canoes, which had been
drawn up on the bank of the Pigeon River for Mackenzie's
inspection.

The fur trade, of course, had always been dependent
upon the French-Canadian canoeman. Only tough, tireless
voyageurs had the strength and stamina to take hundreds
of tons of goods thousands of miles into the continental
interior. Whether they were *mangeurs du lard* (pork
eaters) manning a *canot de maître* between Montreal and
Grand Portage, or *hommes du nord* (northmen), the élite
canoemen who went into the pays d'en haut in the smaller,
lighter *canot du nord*, they were the indispensable work-
horses of the trade. Their endurance was legendary. It
was commonplace for crews to paddle 40 strokes to the
minute for 15 hours a day, with only two meal breaks in
that time and a few short rest spells of 10 or 15 minutes
each. Canoemen averaged four to six miles an hour in
calm waters and, weather permitting, could keep up this
pace for weeks on end.

To the *engagé*, the salaried voyageur of the fur companies, wind, rain, sleet and snow were all part of the job.
The pay, which varied between £15 and £50 a year, was
pitifully inadequate to his hours of work and the con-

ditions under which he performed them. Yet he thought himself fortunate to receive money and a yearly issue of a blanket, a shirt, a pair of trousers, and a few pounds of twist tobacco. (He received twice as much if he was a northman.) When traversing the two-month run from Montreal to Grand Portage, he greatly relished the plainest of daily rations: a mush of lyed corn, peas, and pork or bacon fat; in the pays d'en haut, he munched happily on pemmican in raw chunks or boiled to make what was called "rubaboo."

Mackenzie thoroughly examined each of the watercraft. He looked inside first to ensure that the wooden frame was sound and that every seam had been freshly caulked with pine gum. He paid particular attention to the birchbark hull. It was maddening to find out after a few hour's paddling that some careless canoeman had overlooked a small tear or had done a poor job of patching.

Pemmican was pounded buffalo meat mixed with that animal's fat.

The famous painting "Shooting the Rapids" by Frances Anne Hopkins (who included herself and her husband in the middle of the canoe). This is the type of canoe that the Nor'Westers used between Montreal and Grand Portage. Explain its size and function.

(The problem was not repairing a leak, a simple enough task, but wasting precious hours ashore drying out soaked cargo.) Then he examined the condition of the trade goods on the river bank — *pièces* (packs) of general merchandise, bales of tobacco, cases of hardware and firearms, sacks of provisions, and kegs of gunpowder and liquor. Voyageurs were famous for the speed with which they portaged, but were also notorious for the careless manner in which they handled their loads at each end of a carrying-place. Every *bourgeois* (wintering partner) had to keep a sharp eye open for torn bales and staved kegs, which as often as not proved to be those containing liquor.

Satisfied by his inspection, Mackenzie gave the order to load up. The canoes were slipped into the water clear of the shallows and held steady by bowman and steersman. Thirty items of cargo were loaded aboard each vessel

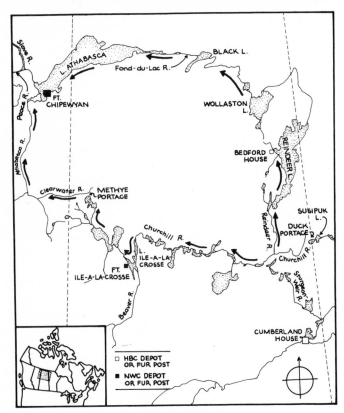

TWO ROUTES INTO ATHABASCA

until there was barely room for each crew to stow themselves and their few belongings.

The "brigade" of canoes set off up the Pigeon River on one of the worst sections of the journey to Pond's base in Athabasca: 600 winding miles through the jumbled granite, dense timber, and lake-strewn wilderness of the Precambrian Shield. This was the "Northwest Road," the historic route into the pays d'en haut.

Fur traders called canoe routes "roads" and referred to canoe trips as "marches."

The Northwest Road duly led Mackenzie over the shallow, wind-tossed waters of Lake Winnipeg to its northwestern corner, where the Saskatchewan River has its exit. Inevitably, there was a long portage near its mouth. Moving briskly upriver, the brigade soon caught sight of Cumberland House, the great inland depot of their rivals, the men from the Hudson's Bay Company. Here, Mackenzie and his men swung north to reach Churchill waters. Several weeks and several hundred miles later, they arrived in what fur traders called the Athabasca country.

Pond's base, a few log huts clustered together near the Athabasca River, occupied a tiny clearing in the vast, dark northern forest of jack pine, spruce, and white birch. The post seemed no different from dozens of others in the pays d'en haut. But there was one significant difference: the location had been very carefully chosen. Pond's base was as deep in the Northwest as was practicable. Athabasca fur brigades had only five months between break-up and freeze-up to canoe and portage the 1,500 miles to and from their special supply depot at Rainy Lake House (several hundred miles northwest of Grand Portage). In addition, the nearby delta of the Athabasca provided fish in abundance to maintain the fort's inhabitants through the long, savage winter.

Roughly three-quarters of the way through the "General History" Mackenzie ends the description of his journey to Athabasca, and in the rest of the *Voyages* there is only one further, brief mention of Peter Pond. This is an amazing omission because there was no one else on earth who could have given Mackenzie the geographical information, rough as it was, on which he was to base both his day-to-day operation of Company affairs in Athabasca and his own explorations. No one else had collected such a mass of geographical facts and speculations, largely because of a desire to solve the

problem that had fascinated trader-explorers since the
time of Champlain: a water route to the "Western Sea,"
the Pacific Ocean.

We will never know exactly why Mackenzie ignores
Pond and his achievements, but it is not hard to make a
few guesses. As indicated earlier, Pond does not seem to
have been an amiable man. And he must have been soured
by the knowledge that after 26 years in the trade, of which
14 had been spent in the western interior, he still held
only one share in a company in which his colleague, with
only three winters' experience to his credit, also possessed
a share. In short, Pond would not be the easiest of companions with whom to share the confined life of a fur
post in winter. As for Mackenzie, he had more than his
share of pride. He seems to have been convinced that he
made his way in the trade without help from anyone; the
"General History" gives no other impression.

Despite Pond's uncertain temper and Mackenzie's
reservations about his colleague's character, the two men
probably managed to get along together. In certain ways
the young Scot and the aging Yankee were curiously alike.
Each was a confident, strong-minded personality. Each
had been remarkably successful in a trade that rewarded
audacity and authority. Lastly, and perhaps most im-
portantly of all, although the reason for Mackenzie's
interest was a quite different one, he came to share Pond's
consuming desire to solve the mysterious geography of
the lands north and west of Athabasca.

During the winter of 1787/88 Pond would explain to
Mackenzie the wide-ranging operations of the Nor'Westers' Athabasca Department. Nine years before, Pond had
found his way into Athabasca via the Methye Portage and
gradually established a network of posts at which highly
successful trading operations were conducted with several
Athapaskan-speaking tribes — Beaver, Chipewyan,
Slave, Dogrib, and Yellowknife. Pond had discovered that
the tributaries and backwaters of the region's two great
waterways, which local Indians called the Athabasca and
Peace Rivers, were breeding grounds for countless
millions of fur-bearing animals and natural highways for
his men to contact Indians along these rivers. And his
traders had found more customers north of Lake Athabasca living beside an extension of the Peace River called
the Slave River, and also along the shores of another huge

body of water, Great Slave Lake, each area being a source of magnificent pelts. But in all likelihood Pond would spend much time talking about the geography of the Northwest, his favourite subject.

Pond had become preoccupied with charting the rivers, mountains, and ultimate boundaries of the regions beyond his post. He may have been stimulated by Indian reports that Russian fur traders had established a trading post somewhere on the Pacific coast of North America. In any case, Pond, a self-taught and talented geographer, was personally curious about the Pacific Ocean. How was it reached overland? What rivers led to the Pacific? And how did the Arctic Ocean fit into the topography of the Northwest?

Pond spent many an Athabasca night trying to piece together the jumbled mixture of what he knew and what he was told, much of which was vague and conflicting. Somehow, he sorted it all out correctly. Pond managed to work out two key facts of the geography of the Northwest. The Athabasca River, which flowed past his post, and the even larger Peace River, which his informants said "descended from the Stony or Rocky Mountains," form the forked tail of a mighty water system that drains northward. Second, that system runs from Lake Athabasca to Great Slave Lake and thence to what Pond called a "mer du Nord West" or "Ice Sea." What Pond plotted on his first map of the Northwest was the exact, main drainage pattern of the Mackenzie River.

The river marked on modern maps as the Mackenzie is the main stream which flows some eleven hundred miles from Great Slave Lake to the Arctic Ocean.

Some time later, perhaps while in Montreal or Quebec City on one of his trips back east, Pond heard of Captain James Cook's epic voyage of 1776 to 1779, the primary purpose of which was to find the Pacific gateway of the fabled Northwest Passage. After he had acquired and studied a copy of the great navigator's text and maps of the voyage, Pond lost all interest in the "Sea of the Northwest" as a possible route to the Pacific. From then on, he complicated the geography of the Northwest and misled both himself and Alexander Mackenzie.

Pond became obsessed by something Cook had observed at one particular location on the north Pacific coast. Cook had found a large estuary that he thought might be "a strait communicating with the northern seas," but it narrowed and "the marks of a river displayed themselves," thick, muddy water "very considerably fresher than any we had hitherto tasted" and full of "large trees and all manner of dirt and rubbish." This estuary, now known as Cook Inlet, has at its eastern end (near the site of modern Anchorage, Alaska) a complex of minor waterways that the great navigator took to be "a great river," which was later officially named "Cook's River" in his honour.

To Pond, this suggested the exit of a huge waterway that either flowed through or originated in the Athabasca country to the north of his post. The result of this theorizing was yet another Pond map of the Northwest. Clearly identified on this map are Great Slave Lake and a broad waterway flowing a short distance westward from it that ends abruptly in the middle of nowhere — plus a

A modern-day reconstruction of the store in a fur post. The loaf-like items hanging from the roof are carrottes *of leaf tobacco. How many other trading items can you recognize?*

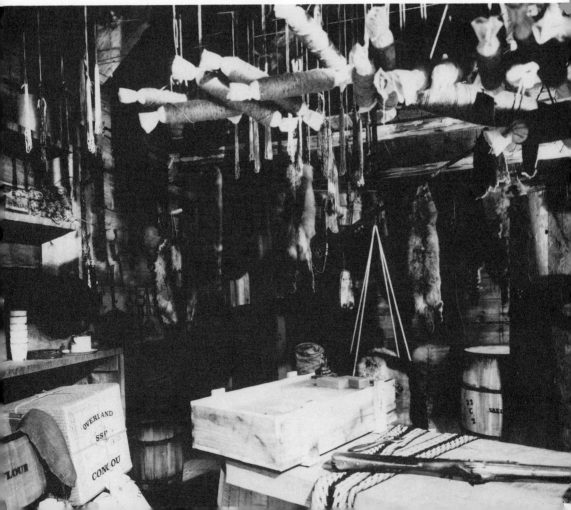

large river marked "Cook's River" that begins equally abruptly in that same stretch of unknown territory and is shown flowing another short distance into Cook Inlet. The implication is obvious. To Pond, these were one and the same waterway.

Unfortunately, like many a man before and after him, Pond was bending facts to fit a theory. There is no water connection between Great Slave Lake and the Pacific. He was right the first time: the waters of the lake flow to the Arctic.

It only remained to prove by exploration that "Cook's River" did lead to and from the Pacific, and perhaps Pond planned to do this. But in the spring of 1788 he handed over the Athabasca Department to Mackenzie and left the pays d'en haut forever. It is not clear why Pond made this decision. (We know so little about individual eighteenth-century fur traders that ninety-nine times out of a hundred we have to guess at the motives of even the more famous among them.) Whatever his reason, or reasons, it is recorded that he sold his single share in the Company and retired, first to Quebec City, and then to his native Connecticut.

The year that Pond left the pays d'en haut Mackenzie had his cousin Roderick officially transferred to the Athabasca Department to supervise the construction of a new trading centre on the southern shore of Lake Athabasca. Trade with the tribes of the area was steadily increasing, and Fort Chipewyan, as the new depot was called, was a much more central location for many customers than Pond's post.

Mackenzie seems to have had some difficulty persuading his cousin to accept the transfer. Roderick had long been disgusted by the sordid, mercenary nature of the trade and was on the point of quitting to seek some other livelihood in Montreal or Quebec City. Alexander had failed several times to convince him that the financial rewards of a partnership would make up for much of the drudgery — "slavery" as Roderick termed it — of a clerk's life in the pays d'en haut. Finally, the "Dear Rory" of their correspondence was persuaded to remain in the trade. Alexander mentioned the likelihood of his going off to explore a route to the Pacific Ocean and begged Roderick to run the department for him in his absence.

Every depot and many a fur post had a kitchen garden like the one shown here. Why?

The First Chapter 4
Exploration, 1789

When Alexander Mackenzie set out in June 1789 on his first voyage, he had no idea he was going to end up at the wrong ocean.

Years afterwards, the shock and humiliation of not quickly discovering an overland route to the Pacific were still so vivid that, at least publicly, he was unable to admit his error. In the Preface to the *Voyages*, he implies that his aim was to prove or disprove the existence of the fabled Northwest Passage between Europe and Asia:

The first voyage has settled the dubious point of a practicable North-West Passage; and I trust it has set that long agitated question at rest and extinguished the disputes respecting it for ever.

This was certainly the result of the voyage. His *purpose* is clearly stated in a private report he sent to Lord Dorchester, Governor General and Commander-in-Chief of British North America, some years after the Arctic voyage:

I followed the course of the waters which had been reported by Mr. Pond to fall into Cook's River; they led me to the Northern Ocean, in latitude 69$^1/_2$ North and about 135 of West Longitude .... It proved that Mr. Pond's assertion was nothing but conjecture, and that a North West passage is impracticable.

Mackenzie was not interested in geographical discovery for its own sake. The motive behind his two explorations was a strongly economic one. The North West Company wanted to find a navigable waterway to the Pacific coast so that trade goods and furs could be shipped cheaply, and in bulk, between Europe and the Northwest instead of being hauled at great expense in canoeloads over the many miles of wilderness waters between Montreal and Grand Portage and then between that depot and all the many posts in the pays d'en haut. And Mackenzie fully agreed with the logic behind this thinking. An inexpensive supply route by sea was the basic strength of the Hudson's Bay Company, together with the fact that its main depots on the Bay (Churchill Factory and York Factory) were farther north and west than Grand Portage. His years in a counting house in Montreal had shown him that fur trading was financed by borrowing enormous amounts of money in the form of trade goods. His early years in the interior convinced him how dangerous — if not insane — it was to expose this capital to the vagaries of rock and rapid.

As he stresses in the *Voyages*, transport to and from the most distant parts of Athabasca

> . . . occupies an extent of from three to four thousand miles through upwards of sixty large lakes and numerous rivers, and the means of transport are slight bark canoes. It must also be observed that these waters are intercepted by more than two hundred rapids, along which the articles of merchandise are chiefly carried on men's backs and over an hundred and thirty carrying-places, from twenty-five paces to thirteen miles in length . . . .

This fantastically long, fantastically expensive transport route — to which must be added another 3,000-mile haul of goods from and furs to Britain — was the reason why the margin of profit over cost was never very great in the Montreal fur trade. In fact, Mackenzie estimated that the cost of transportation was half the total cost of carrying on the trade. It is true that a few men made fortunes in the trade but only "by penny pinching and a driving of the voyageurs to a degree that would horrify a modern trade union."

Mackenzie, an exceedingly profit-minded Scot, was determined to lessen the tremendous imbalance between expenditure and income in the fur trade. His first attempt to do so was the voyage of 1789.

Mackenzie's account of that voyage begins in typi-cally matter-of-fact fashion: "Wednesday, June 3. At 9 o'clock embarked at Fort Chipewyan." The explorer shared his canoe with four French Canadians, two of whom had brought their Indian wives along, and a German. An Indian, who had acquired the title of English Chief because of a former lengthy connection with the HBC, and his two wives travelled in a separate, smaller canoe; and a couple of young Indians, followers of the chief, accompanied the party in a third. The voyageurs were Joseph Landry, Charles Ducette, François Barrieau, Pierre de Lorme, and John Steinbruck.

It has been said that the culture of Indians living in the subarctic reflects their eternal need to survive a harsh environment. How do these illustrations back up this statement?

Mackenzie had supervised the construction of his own canoe. It was 32 feet long and designed to carry 25 pièces of goods, a few bags of pemmican and of corn as emergency rations, and a crew of four and their gear. In addition to the customary iron-shod punting poles, and towing lines, each of the watercraft was provided with a mast and a sail of double-sewn canvas. Mackenzie personally checked the quantity and quality of the repair materials being taken along. He paid particular attention to the cloths soaked in oil and animal fat that were the makeshift waterproofing laid over the cargoes of trade goods. Then he doublechecked that the canoes carried the spare muskets and extra shot and powder he had ordered.

On each of his explorations Mackenzie hoarded his supplies of pemmican and corn and fed his party off the countryside as much as possible. As soon as the party had landed for the night, he and his hunters usually went off in search of game for the supper pot, or to acquire supplies of duck, goose, or deer for consumption the following day. If game was scarce, no northman refused a meal of fish, particularly the rich, firm flesh of the whitefish, which was easily netted in large quantities and quickly broiled over the campfire.

The party was soon on the broad, silt-laden waters of the Slave River, which is the name the Peace River assumes as it journeys north of Lake Athabasca. For the next few days the weather was rainy, chilly, and blowy. The rain became so heavy and the wind so violent that Mackenzie was forced to remain encamped beside the river. Finally, at 2:30 one foggy morning, Mackenzie roused his men and set off downstream again. By nine o'clock they had reached Great Slave Lake, where everyone suddenly felt a biting chill in the air. The huge lake was entirely covered with ice, except close to the shore.

Held up for several days until drenching rainstorms and blustery winds had broken up the ice, Mackenzie had plenty of time to observe his surroundings. He noted the considerable permafrost condition: the ground, a mixture of clay and sand, had thawed out to a depth of only 18 inches and thus prevented any noticeable growth of plant life except trees. However, the region was rich in wildlife. Unfortunately, the wildlife also included a large insect population. Mackenzie remarks that, upon the weather becoming clear with westerly winds, his party encountered "old companions," mosquitoes which "visit us in greater numbers than we would wish as they are very troublesome guests."

Dodging hurriedly from island to island, it took the party a whole week to cross a 35-mile stretch of Great Slave Lake to its north shore. Despite high winds and torrential rainstorms, the men managed to prevent their frail canoes from being crushed by rampaging ice floes or ripped open by sheet ice, which formed rapidly even in late June. When Mackenzie landed on the barren, rocky north shore and met three lodges of Yellowknives, he sent one of them off to fetch the members of other lodges living close by. These Indians offered him beaver and marten skins but could not give him what he really wanted — positive information about the river that emptied out of the lake's western end. However, one Yellowknife thought that he'd seen the beginnings of such a waterway and was immediately engaged as the party's guide. Ever the business-minded Scot, Mackenzie lectured the group sternly on the benefits it would derive from trapping and promised a trading post, which would be maintained "as long as they would deserve it."

This illustration clearly shows the stark landscape of the Canadian North. The photograph is a composite of thirteen exposures taken of the "midnight sun." On his voyage to the Arctic, Mackenzie tried (without much success) to share with his voyageurs the wonders of discovery — the strange flora and fauna beyond the Arctic Circle, and the phenomenon of the midnight sun.

How do you explain a sun that does not disappear below the horizon?

It was on June 27 that their guide directed them into a
deep bay, which he thought might be the entrance to the
river. But its waters lacked any clear sign of a current and
brought them up against masses of broken ice, whose
presence was made even more menacing by slowly drift-
ing patches of fog. Backpaddling very carefully, the
explorers finally found refuge for the night on a nearby
island. They suffered the same disappointment the
following day after they had coursed down a long bay
that led westward. This time the guide assured them that
they would arrive at the river. But after hours of paddling,
the canoes scraped to a halt in shallow waters. English
Chief, in a passion of rage, promptly threatened to shoot
the Yellowknife. Mackenzie doesn't say whether or not
fear improved a lazy memory, but at this point the guide
suddenly recalled journeying from the river through
wooded country to the very spot where the canoes were
now beached.

The guide was right — or a lucky guesser. The party
broke camp at four the next morning, backtracked out of
the bay, rounded yet another headland, and soon detected
a strong, smooth current taking them out of Great Slave
Lake. Later that day, a stiff breeze from the east drove
them downriver under sail at a very brisk rate. Mackenzie
must have been elated: having fixed Great Slave as being
at 61°40′N — approximately the latitude of "Cook's
River" — he was now on a major waterway leading westward. On July 3, he calculated that they had run downstream 217 miles west and 44 miles north. Sooner or later
he expected the river to pierce the Rockies and lead to the
Pacific.

However, as day succeeded day, the river flowed
steadily northwest, and the mountains always remained
tantalizingly at a distance to the west. Early on the
morning of July 5 in the neighbourhood of modern Fort
Norman, Mackenzie received a faint hint about where he
was heading. He went ashore to speak with a small group
of Slaves and Dogribs. Their vague information about the
river "had so much of the fabulous" about it that he
ignored the kernel of truth in their statement that the
explorers would be several winters getting to "the sea."
English Chief and his men were much depressed by this
information because they were already tired of the
voyage and also feared that the farther north the party

*Mackenzie continually
underestimated the force of
the current: the party averaged 100 miles a day going
downstream.*

advanced, the scarcer game would become. But Mackenzie persuaded them otherwise and even induced them to bribe a Dogrib with presents of kettles, an axe, and a knife to join the party.

VOYAGE TO THE ARCTIC, 1789

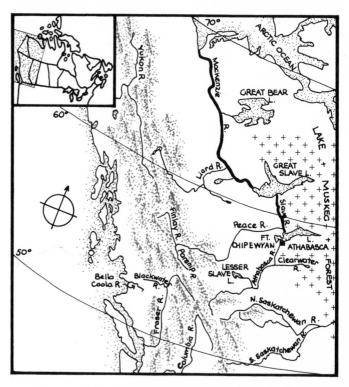

By July 10, his observations told him he was at "67.47 North latitude, which is farther north than I had expected." According to the sun and his sextant, he was nowhere near Cook's River and was clearly not on one of its tributaries. And a Hare guide he had picked up along the way to replace the obviously desertion-minded Dogrib knew of no river other than the one on which they were travelling. According to his information, Mackenzie would come in ten days to the sea and three days later meet with Eskimos who had formerly made war upon the Hares. Even the landscape suggested a huge delta, because they had now come to a region where the river widened enormously and filtered its way through channels banked with mud and sand, which were so various that "we were at a loss what channel out of some hundred to take."

Mackenzie spent several days in the river delta dodging fogbanks and ice floes while trying to establish its northernmost extent. He wasn't even sure that he'd reached Pond's "Ice Sea," despite a rise in the water level one night. On the 15th, the water again rose during the early hours and soaked the baggage, and this time he was forced to admit that "as the wind had not changed nor blew harder than when we went to bed, we were all of the opinion that it was the tide." He had come to the Hyperborean Sea, as he often termed Arctic waters.

The brief northern summer was almost over, and he was unable to advance northward or westward. In addition, his supply of provisions was running dangerously low and he had 13 hungry followers to feed. There was nothing to do but backtrack as quickly as possible before winter imprisoned them all somewhere along the hundreds of miles between the Arctic Ocean and Fort Chipewyan.

Short of food and time, Mackenzie pushed his men hard, and the return journey severely tested their strength and stamina. For much of it they were forced to "track" or haul the canoes by means of shoulder harnesses attached to bow and stern, which meant either ploughing through river debris in the shallows or stumbling painfully over stones and boulders as they waded breast-high through icy water. The weather still varied wildly from oppressively hot days to ones on which bitingly cold winds swept down from the Arctic "and we can't put clothes enough on to keep us warm." Yet the men averaged 30 miles a day going upstream, and the party was back at Fort Chipewyan in just under two months, having completed in 102 days a round trip of almost 3,000 miles, the equivalent of a direct coast-to-coast journey between Halifax, Nova Scotia, and Vancouver, British Columbia. The river section of the voyage was itself a fantastic performance on the part of the northmen, who had made the downward run in 14 days but took only 38 days to fight their way back against the unrelenting current.

Mackenzie does not record his private thoughts as his men laboured upstream on what he is said to have called the "River Disappointment." But he was still determined to find a way to "Cook's River." And it was in the course of his return from Arctic tidewater that Mackenzie first heard echoes of Europeans on the Pacific. The first occasion was when a band of Indians recounted

This watery maze of lake, pond, slough, and swamp is a typical scene in the Mackenzie River delta. Is the river "good" for anything today?

an Eskimo report of meeting white men "in large canoes" far to the westward "eight or ten winters since" and exchanging leather for iron. (This contact might have been with Captain Cook but was more likely with Russian traders somewhere on the northwest coast of Alaska.) Some days later he talked with a Dogrib, who repeated a Hare Indian story of a mighty river on the other side of the western mountains that fell into the "White Man's Lake" far to the northwest. The Dogrib said that the Indians who lived at the river mouth made "canoes larger than ours," which tallied with Cook's descriptions of Pacific coast dugouts and war canoes, and killed "a kind of large beaver, the skin of which is almost red," which was unmistakably a description of the sea otter.

The only reason Mackenzie didn't clamber up and over the mountains right there and then was that the Indian refused the explorer's attempts to hire him as a guide. So Mackenzie simply had to accept the bitter fact that he had not found a way to the Pacific. The expedition had been a total failure — or so he thought. But then Mackenzie had no way of knowing that he had explored and charted the North American river that is exceeded in length only by the mighty Mississippi River system.

The Second Exploration, 1793

Mackenzie remarked in a letter to Roderick that at the July 1790 meeting of the partners at Grand Portage, "My Expedition is hardly spoken of but this is what I expected." It had not led to the Pacific.

The voyage, however, did have important results. It proved that there was no practicable route to the Pacific in high latitudes. Even at the height of the northern summer, there was no way westward through the Arctic ice. Secondly, Mackenzie had demolished a great historic myth by demonstrating that there was no northwest passage through the continent. Thirdly, he had discovered that the "River Disappointment" itself ran through several thousand square miles of fur-rich territory. Lastly, the basic reason for his journey held good because a way to the Pacific still had to be found.

Long after his return to Athabasca, Mackenzie decided that the Pacific could be reached by the "Great River which falls into the Sea to the Westward of the river in which I voyaged." The only trouble was that the more he questioned Indians, the more he seemed to hear of *two* great rivers beyond the Rocky Mountains: they were variously described as the "Great River of the West" and the "river that runs towards the midday sun." (Mackenzie must have been getting bits and pieces of information about what we now call the Columbia and the Fraser. At this time, no European suspected that there were *two* great river systems west of the mountains.) Evidently both waterways led to the "White Man's Lake," but did so far to the south of Athabasca's latitude. Yet the reports were so often confusing that Mackenzie decided he was really hearing about one large waterway. In any case, there was no denying the large flow of fresh water at the end of Cook Inlet, and there were strong reports of a river running northwest in the general direction of the inlet. Logically, he stood a better chance of reaching the west

Knives, to which crude lengths of wood, short or long, could be fitted, were extremely popular trading items. In fact, they were used almost as much by a trader's men as by his customers.

Why were knives so popular with customers?

coast by going up the Peace River and seeking what Pond had described as "Cook's River."

Late in 1792, Mackenzie prepared for his second attempt to find a water route to and from the Pacific. If he was going to get to the Pacific and back in the course of a summer season, the nearer the ocean he started, the better. After wintering as far up the Peace as possible, he would make a quick dash westward and hurry back to Fort Chipewyan before winter closed in again. As before, the faithful Roderick would stand in for him at Fort Chipewyan.

Mackenzie's tiny brigade of three canoes paddled away across the choppy, green waters of Lake Athabasca on the morning of October 10. Two days later they turned westward into the mile-wide, muddy mouth of the Peace River. They had to hurry along: the weather was bitterly cold, and ice formed on the river every night. For several days he drove his voyageurs hard. On November 1, they managed to reach the place that had been chosen as wintering quarters, a site five or six miles west along the Peace from its junction with the Smoky (the site of modern Peace River, Alberta). Awaiting Mackenzie were two men who had been sent ahead in the spring to square timbers and cut palisades, and a large number of Indians. Mackenzie called the tribesmen to him and gave each about four inches of tobacco and a dram of spirits. Then he told them he would treat them kindly — if they brought in the furs that he expected from them. To this end, he spent the next six days equipping the Indians for their winter hunting and also arranging for the provisioning of his post with fresh meat. Only when this was done did Mackenzie give his full attention to the construction of Fort Fork, and it was almost Christmas before he was able to move out of his tent and into the hut erected for him.

The new year was only a few days old when two Beaver Indians turned up at Fort Fork with the information that just beyond the mountains was a great waterway running towards the midday sun. They also informed Mackenzie that all the way to the mountains the countryside of the Peace was abundant with animals. These seemed omens of success. But two events a few months later bitterly disappointed him. The local Indians proved to be poor trappers: early in May he had only six

canoeloads of furs to send back to Fort Chipewyan. And
Mackenzie had had great trouble securing guides. At one
point, he managed to engage three. However, one, who
claimed to have been on a very large river two days' march
west of the mountains, deserted the day before Mackenzie
left, and "the two remaining lads knew no more of the
country than I do myself."

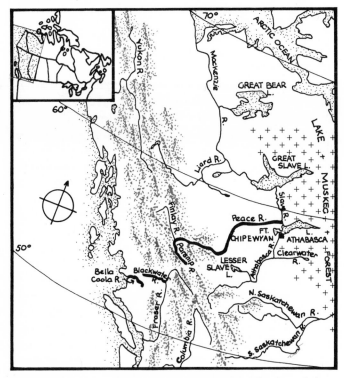

*VOYAGE TO THE
PACIFIC, 1793*

   Mackenzie was also greatly troubled by doubts of the
wisdom of what he was attempting. In a letter to Roderick
penned the night before he set off, he wrote first that
matters were "too far advanced not to make some
attempt." Farther on, he confessed:

I never was so undecided in my intentions as this year regarding
my going to the [Grand] Portage or remaining inland. I weighed
everything in my mind over and over again .... I begin to think it
is the height of folly in a man to reside in a country of this kind,
deprived of every comfort that can render life agreeable, especially
when he has a competency to enjoy life in civilized society ...
   Yours unchangeably,

The loneliness of command, which his own reserved
manner did nothing to improve, and the isolation of a

frontier post in winter were beginning to affect his nerves and his judgment. In addition, he was probably nervous at the thought of again taking off into the unknown. But of course he would go on, driven by his determination to succeed.

On the evening of May 9, 1793, Mackenzie set off west up the Peace River. He took with him as his second-in-command, Alexander McKay, a Nor'Wester clerk, six voyageurs — two of whom, Joseph Landry and Charles Ducette, had accompanied him to the Arctic — and two Indian guides. They all travelled in a canoe built to Mackenzie's specifications. It was large enough to carry the ten men (and a dog) and 3,000 pounds of provisions, goods, ammunition, and baggage, yet on an easy portage two men could carry it for three miles without resting.

Some days later, they approached a section of the river that Indians had warned Mackenzie was a succession of rapids, cascades, and falls, which were always avoided by a portage north of the river. Mackenzie disregarded the warning and directed his men up the south side of the canyon. After towing the heavily loaded canoe for about a mile, the party was forced by overhanging rock to cross over to the north side, where stones loosened by spring thaws and recent rains were continually rolling down into the Peace. The river bank itself was steep, and the men were having trouble enough finding their footing without being knocked off balance by falling debris or having stones slide out from under their moccasined feet. In the course of the next two miles, the rapids were so bad that the party — including Mackenzie — had to portage the canoe's contents no less than five times.

For three exhausting days they fought the Peace River, until "it began to be muttered on all sides that there was no alternative but to return." Yet for all their labours, when Mackenzie climbed part way up the side of the canyon he could see nothing but a steady succession of rapids and falls within an ever widening canyon. Since the water route was impassible, Mackenzie struck off across country over what turned out to be a seven-mile mountain trail. It was a good job that he did. It took them three days to carry the canoe and all its baggage up, over, and down Portage Mountain, but Mackenzie and his men would never have survived the maelstrom of mad waters in the horseshoe-shaped canyon of the Peace.

In the foreground
is the upper (western) end
of the Peace River Canyon
as it looked in Mackenzie's
day. (It has since been
radically changed by the
construction of a power
dam.) In the background,
jutting out from the north
bank, is the spit of land
where Mackenzie and his
men ended the long haul
up and over Portage Moun-
tain.

Many rivers originate
within the Rocky Mountains.
Some flow westward, some
northward, and some eastward.
Why do they go in three
different directions?
Where will the
waters in this
photograph
end up?

May 19, the day they first entered the Peace Canyon, must have been an experience that shattered the men's self-confidence. Hitherto, they had mastered all the waters of the pays d'en haut. But they had never encountered the fury and menace of a mountain river in flood, particularly one which, as even Mackenzie admitted, was "one white sheet of foaming water." After the traverse around the canyon, Mackenzie kept his terrified, near-mutinous men moving westward for weeks on his own reserves of will power and courage. The only thing *he* feared was failure to complete his mission.

As they journeyed westward some days later, snow-capped peaks towered on either side of them — the Rocky Mountains. It was almost the end of May and the sun shone clearly, but the dry cold of the region was so penetrating that even the hardy voyageurs complained of their numb hands as they worked the poles. In fact, the weather was so bitter that the men had to wear their blanket coats day and night. To keep them good-humoured, Mackenzie gave them a daily *regale* (tot of rum), and by May 29 a whole keg had been consumed.

By May 31, they had passed through the Rocky Mountains and come to what in later years was called Finlay Forks, where the Finlay River, racing down the Rocky Mountain Trench from the northwest, joined the Parsnip River from the southeast to form the Peace River. West of the Forks was a chain of mountains "running south and north as far as the eye could reach." Which waterway were they to take?

The Finlay led north and looked easier, and the men made it plain that it was their choice. Mackenzie agreed "as it appeared to me to be the most likely to bring us nearest to the part where I wished to fall on the Pacific Ocean." But he recalled that an aged Beaver warrior he had met earlier that year at Fork York had advised him

> ... not on any account to follow it [the Finlay], as it was soon lost in various branches among the mountains, and that there was no great river that ran in any direction near it; but by following the latter [the Parsnip], we should arrive at a carrying-place to another large river, that did not exceed a day's march, where the inhabitants build houses and live upon islands . . . .

He ordered the steersmen to proceed up the swifter, narrower Parsnip. It was a crucial decision. The Finlay would have led the party to where the headwaters of the

Liard, Skeena, and Stikine Rivers interlock in a maze of
streams; in all likelihood they would have lost their way
completely. Very sensibly, Mackenzie heeded the old
man's warning, although as a result he had to endure days
of bitter complaint from his men and, worse still, occa-
sional doubts as to the wisdom of his choice.

Eight days upstream from Finlay Forks, Mackenzie
became desperately anxious to find the carrying-place
that the aged Beaver had said would take him to "the
large river ... where the inhabitants build houses and live
upon islands." Late that night, over a supper of boiled
wild parsnips and pemmican, Mackenzie fretted about
the location of the carrying-place. Had he actually seen it
and mistaken it for one of the numerous island channels
on the river? Did it exist at all?

On June 9, guided by a local Sekani Indian, they left
the main stream of the Parsnip behind and traversed a
two-mile-long body of water (Arctic Lake). A brief
journal entry for June 12 notes:

We landed and unloaded, where we found a beaten path leading
over a low ridge of land of eight hundred and seventeen paces in
length to another small lake [Portage Lake].

In portaging these 817 paces to the second lake,
Mackenzie and his followers had crossed the continental
divide. They had left behind them waters draining ultimately into the Arctic. For the first time they were, in
Mackenzie's words, "going with the stream." They were
on water that would find its way to the Pacific Ocean.

Once across a third body of water (Pacific Lake) and
a third portage, they came to a turbulent, ice-cold stream
(James Creek), which Mackenzie would have good reason
to name Bad River. In the course of the first day on its
shallow, upper waters, they spent about as much time
clearing away fallen trees and easing their craft over
banks of gravel as they did canoeing. They had barely got
under way the next morning when a surge of the current
drove their craft sideways down the river and broke its
back on a gravel bar. Driven on into deeper water by the
stream's swift flow, the canoe was thrust against a large
boulder, which shattered the stern. The violence of this
contact hurled the craft across the river, where its bow
was crushed by rocks. Carried on over a cascade, the
canoe had several large holes torn in it and many of its

ribs broken. At Mackenzie's curt command, the crew tumbled out of the wreck into the water but held fast to the gunwales. Several hundred yards later, waterlogged but afloat, the canoe grounded in shallow water, and the badly shaken, half-frozen crew staggered to their feet. Somehow, no one had been injured.

Mackenzie first made sure that his men's spirits were revived: a roaring fire was built, a hearty meal eaten, and a generous slug of rum was drunk all round. Then he used his great powers of persuasion, appealing particularly to their loyalty and to their pride. His speech had the intended effect. One of the Indians found enough bark, poor in quality though it was, to patch up the worst gashes in their craft, and oilcloth was used to repair the minor holes. The job took two days. By the time they had finished, the canoe was held together almost as much by gum as by fabric.

They started off again on the clear, warm morning of June 15, plagued every step of their way by mosquitoes and sand flies. It took the party 14 hours to travel three miles, but the canoe survived several dangerous places and remained afloat. The next day they had to portage around several falls, first through a swamp, then in mud that was hip-deep, and finally through a seemingly endless tangle of fallen trees and thick underbrush. By seven in the evening Mackenzie and his followers had managed to advance two miles. To complete their miseries, the Sekani guide stole away in the early hours of the next morning.

June 17 was spent hacking a way back to the creek, floating the canoe downstream until large amounts of driftwood made this too dangerous, and then hauling everything along the banks of the river, which soon branched into various small unnavigable channels. Once again they found themselves forced to carry the canoe and all its contents through swampy ground. But at eight in the evening, to their inexpressible joy, they came to the east bank of a navigable waterway (the headwaters of the Fraser River between Herrick Creek and McGregor River). By way of celebration, Mackenzie allowed his men to sleep in until seven in the morning, but by eight the party was afloat again on waters driven along by a strong current. That day they came to "the great fork, of which our guide had informed us" (the fork formed by the McGregor and Fraser Rivers).

On June 21, somewhere about 20 miles below the junction of the Quesnel and Fraser Rivers, Mackenzie landed to question some Salish Indians as to how best to get to the Pacific. The next day he did the same thing with other Indians, and was intrigued enough by their frank, friendly reception to stay for a whole day of questions and answers. On the 23rd, after a restless night, he made the second major decision of the voyage.

Mackenzie had to consider several matters. He had provisions for only 30 days, and the sole food reserve was a 90-pound bag of pemmican he had cached three days before. Supplementing this with game would be difficult because, in the course of the battering the canoe had received on James Creek, much of their stock of musket balls had been lost. Unless he could barter for food, or his Indian guides proved unduly skilful with bow and arrow, the party would have to go on short rations. Yet he was determined to return to Fort Chipewyan before winter set in. He could not ignore his Athabasca responsibilities.

In the left background is Mount Robson, the highest peak (12,972 ft.) in the Canadian Rockies. Down its steep, southern slope plunges the meltwater of snow and ice to feed, via the Robson River (foreground), the young Fraser River.

When Mackenzie first came to Fraser waters, a few miles from this scene, he noted in his journals that "the current was very slack" and that the channel was only sixteen feet deep. If he had gone on down the Fraser all the way to its mouth, would he have found a navigable route to the Pacific?

An equally strong factor in his decision was his growing conviction that the river flowing past his encampment was not "Cook's River." He calculated that he should have come across it somewhere about 56°N, yet his calculations indicated that he was now just a little south of 52°N on a waterway that apparently ran far to the south. It was probably the "Great River of the West" he had heard of from so many Indians. (In later years he decided that it was the Columbia; it was, as another later Nor'Wester discovered, the Fraser.) Thus he would have to backtrack and find the waterway he was to name the West Road River* that, as local Indians said, led to the "lake whose water is nauseous."

He addressed his men in a frank, determined manner, commending their "fortitude, patience, and perseverance." But he stressed that he would reach the sea either by an overland journey to the west or, if a guide failed to make this possible, by returning to where they now were and going downriver to its mouth, whatever the distance. The self-control of the men had been slowly giving way to the fear and panic that, in the wilderness, means death. But Mackenzie's continuous display of confidence and determination were, to his voyageurs, the only certain things in an uncertain world. They responded to his leadership, unanimously agreeing to follow wherever he might go. In so doing, they paid him the finest of compliments.

Mackenzie found his guide, and the remainder of his westward journey is yet another example of his unshakable will to reach the Pacific: the return some distance upriver in the "crazy vessel," which finally proved unrepairable and had to be replaced by building another from scratch and caching it for their return; the winding ascent into the cold, cloudy, blue-and-white world of the coastal mountains; the slogging march of almost two weeks through uplands sodden with rain and the meltwater of snow and ice; the descent into the lush, sheltered valley of the Bella Coolas, who worshipped and ate the salmon; and, on July 20, the arrival at Pacific waters.

Two days later, he wrote in his journal:

I now mixed up some vermilion in melted grease and inscribed in large characters, on the southeast face of the rock on which we

Known for many years since as the Blackwater River.

As Mackenzie himself discovered, the Indians of the North Pacific Coast were nearly always well-fed and also rich in material possessions.
    Why was food plentiful? What sort of possessions did these people have?

had slept last night, this brief memorial — "Alexander Mackenzie, from Canada, by land, the twenty-second of July, one thousand seven hundred and ninety-three."

By various observations during the day and night of the 22nd, Mackenzie established his position as 128° 2′ West of Greenwich and 52° 20′ 48″ North. Then — and only then — did he give the word to McKay and the jittery, weary voyageurs to turn back eastward.

In the Preface to the *Voyages* Mackenzie says that his second exploration was

. . . to determine the practicability of a commercial communication through the continent of North America between the Atlantic and Pacific Oceans, which is proved by my second journal.

He had certainly proved that such communication was possible. But, in terms of practicability, he had proved exactly the opposite. No birchbark craft could survive the raging mountain waters he had traversed, least of all a canoe that would be laden to the gunwales with trade goods or bales of furs. He himself had only got to the Pacific after abandoning his own canoe, making a *two-week* portage, and then borrowing a canoe from local Indians. Mackenzie had failed to find a navigable route to and from the Pacific through the confusing jumble of mountain ranges between the Rockies and the coast. But his characteristically stubborn refusal to accept defeat from man and nature alike made his failure a triumph.

The Historic Sites and Monuments Board of Canada has erected a monument and tablet to mark the terminus of Mackenzie's journey to the Pacific. The board also had this famous inscription carved on the rock and filled with reddened cement.

Chapter 6 A Nor'Wester Agent

The return journey was not without incident. At the start Mackenzie nearly lost his life when he was mobbed by Indians at a place he afterwards termed "Rascals' Village." He was only saved by the accident of one of his voyageurs appearing on the scene, which caused the natives to flee. But this shaky beginning was more than offset by the discovery that their new canoe was intact where they had stored it at the junction of the West Road River and the Fraser; and the pemmican they had cached was untouched. In addition, game proved to be plentiful, particularly once they were back on the Peace. This was most fortunate, because on one occasion the carcass of a 250-pound elk lasted only three meals, being "consumed by ten persons and a large dog, who was allowed his share of the banquet."

Mackenzie's journal of his voyage to the Pacific ends with the information that "after an absence of eleven months, I arrived at Fort Chipewyan, where I remained for the purposes of trade during the succeeding winter." It proved to be a bad season for him.

By March 1794, he was confessing to Roderick that

... I never passed so much of my time insignificantly, nor so uneasily. Although I am not superstitious, dreams among other things caused me much annoyance. I could not close my eyes without finding myself in company with the dead.

He had taken too much out of himself in the summer of 1793 and was now paying the price of deep physical exhaustion and of a serious mental depression that was largely the result of the primitive, isolated life he had long loathed. What Mackenzie craved above all else was the civilized world beyond Athabasca, specifically Montreal, where trade policies and decisions were made. He had to be part of that world, and in 1794 he left Fort Chipewyan with this intention firmly in his mind.

As it happened, Mackenzie was destined to leave the

pays d'en haut that year, never to return farther west than Lake Superior.

The explorer found a pleasant surprise awaiting him when he came "out" with the Athabasca brigades and arrived at Grand Portage in the summer of 1794. No complaint was made about the wages and supplies that the Pacific expedition had cost the Company. Nor were there any grumbles that the exploration had not made practicable the immediate exploitation of new fur regions. Instead, he was complimented on displaying great fortitude in seeking new business, which was more and more becoming a prime objective of the Company. The Nor'Westers had had to take in several new members, which diminished share values and therefore made the Company anxious to increase annual returns. Competition, or rather an open threat of competition, had been levelled at the Nor'Westers, principally from the old Montreal firm of Todd, McGill & Co. and the new one of Forsyth, Richardson & Co. When a formal agreement had been drawn up in 1792 in order to buy off both Todd, McGill and Forsyth, Richardson by giving them a few shares, the explorer had been allotted no less than six shares in an expanded 46-share North West Company.

Mackenzie's name does not appear in the 1795 list of North West Company partners, except as "agent and Attorney" for the winterers. He had been made a co-partner and agent of McTavish, Frobisher & Company, a firm that had become the virtual directorate of the North West Company. Mackenzie was ordered to report to Montreal. The Nor'Westers needed his bold, forceful ways of doing things at headquarters.

While there was much work for the new agent to do, Montreal gave him ample opportunity to enjoy himself. He was now "Nor'West Mackenzie," a much admired member of a group of people who delighted in giving dinner or supper parties and needed no excuse to organize dances and balls. One of his copartners, Joseph Frobisher, was host to many gatherings of notables, including some of the important military and administrative officials of what, in 1791, had become the Province of Lower Canada. The senior partner, Simon McTavish, probably the richest man in Montreal at this time, had recently married, set up house in rue Saint-Jean-Baptiste, and was much given to entertaining. Mackenzie himself shared comfortable bachelor quarters with William McGillivray, his fellow agent and McTavish's nephew, in a house on the lower slope of Mount Royal.

But, despite his growing fame and increasing wealth, Mackenzie was happy with neither his position nor his prospects in McTavish, Frobisher & Co. He was the fifth of five copartners and had little say in determining overall Nor'Wester policy. A long-cherished plan he had to expand, regulate, and control the entire fur trade had not been advanced one whit.

Mackenzie seems to have excited his friend and colleague, Will McGillivray, with his notions of establishing "one common interest" to supervise the trade and to conduct all freighting of goods through Hudson Bay. Mackenzie had even impressed these same ideas on Colonel John Graves Simcoe, Lieutenant-Governor of Upper Canada. On his way to Montreal, Mackenzie had stopped off at Niagara-on-the-Lake to pay his respects to the governor, and they enjoyed a long chat together. Simcoe judged him "as intelligent as he is adventurous" and listened attentively to his proposals. These included the establishment by the British government of two posts on the Pacific coast as a claim to sovereignty, and Simcoe incorporated all this in a long report on western problems that he sent to London. In Simcoe's account is the first intimation of the project that Mackenzie tried to promote over and over again in later years.

> . . . the most practicable Rout to the Northwest was thro' the territories of the Hudson's Bay Company; that by the Rout from Great Britain all the Navigation from Montreal thro' the chain of Lakes & their immense Communication to the most distant part of the interior Country & its consequent Carriage would be saved.

However, nothing came of Simcoe's report. In succeeding years, probably in the course of several visits to England, Mackenzie found out why. His plan of action ran counter to the interests of three well-established commercial monopolies. First, the Hudson's Bay Company possessed by royal charter the exclusive powers of trade and government in those regions whose waters emptied into Hudson Bay, which amounted to the entire pays d'en haut, except Athabasca. Second, the East India Company had a similar charter for much of India, but also possessed the exclusive right of British trade in China, a market American fur entrepreneurs were finding profit-

While the HBC could not oust the Montrealers from the western interior, it did deny them the use of the Bay.

able for sea otter and other furs. The third monopoly belonged to the South Sea Company, which had the right of trade west of Cape Horn. No British vessel could trade beyond the Cape without its permission, which could only be secured by paying a special toll.

Unfortunately, even McGillivray had been unable to promote Mackenzie's grand design within McTavish, Frobisher. Once more competition had been steadily building up in the pays d'en haut and had completely absorbed the day-to-day attention of Mackenzie's co-partners. This time, the opposition to the North West Company refused to be bought off, and the Nor'Westers found themselves facing competent rivals all the way from Grand Portage to Fort Chipewyan.

In the last decade of the eighteenth century the three giants of the Canadian fur trade were the North West Company, Todd, McGill & Company, and Forsyth, Richardson & Company. Among them, they accounted for close to two-thirds of all furs exported from Montreal. But, at the time of a further North West Company re-organization in 1795, Todd & McGill had decided against engaging actively in the northwest trade. Forsyth, Richardson found its proposed share of the arrangement

Trading often involved accepting furs other than beaver, for example, wolf, lynx, or bear, although each of these had a modest market value.

This scene is interesting for two particular reasons. It was quite possibly painted in the days of the French fur trade. And the Indians are offering a solitary pelt, because they were members of a group that was never much interested in fur trading. What group was this? What activities were more rewarding to them than bartering furs?

Of the four Beaver Club medals know to exist, this one belonged to James McGill, one of the first British trader-merchants to operate out of Montreal. One face of the medal confirms that he passed the test of membership — spending at least one winter in the pays d'en haut — as early as 1766. Although not founded until 1785, the club included several men who went west before the fall of New France in 1760. So Alexander Mackenzie was something of a latecomer when elected to membership in 1795.

of 1795 unacceptable and fought back by providing financial backing for various independent traders in the pays d'en haut. In 1798, these men signed a formal agreement with Forsyth, Richardson and the firm of Leith, Jamieson & Company to form the "New North West Company" or, as it was usually called by the Nor'Westers, the XY Company. By 1799, this opposition had penetrated as far inland as Lake Athabasca and set up a trading post near Fort Chipewyan.

Several historians have implied that Mackenzie had some hand in creating the XY group, although there is no proof that he was running with the hares and hunting with the hounds. He seems to have been aware of what was developing. He wrote Roderick in October 1797 of "the formation of a concern against the North West Company by Messrs. Forsyth, Richardson & Company and others," a statement that anticipated by a year the actual legal establishment of the New North West Company. However, this sounds very much like trade gossip. It was not until he wrote his Montreal colleagues in June 1799 from Grand Portage that Mackenzie seems to have gathered any positive information regarding the opposition's corporate structure and personnel. And the letter clearly reads as if he had just found out the first detailed information about the XY Company.

Mackenzie had no reason at this time to change sides. The XY Company had just started to challenge the "wolves of the north." Others had tried and failed to upset the near-monopoly of trade that the Nor'Westers enjoyed in the pays d'en haut. All that is known about Mackenzie at this point in his career is that, in October 1799, he sailed for England aboard the merchantman *Desire*, although his contract with McTavish, Frobisher was due for renewal in December of that year.

Some of Mackenzie's fellow menbers were almost as famous as was he. Alexander Henry (the Elder) and Joseph Frobisher were two such. Simon Fraser was another. Why were they well-known personalities?

Sir Alexander Mackenzie

In the long history of the fur trade, there are few more puzzling episodes than the break in 1799 between Alexander Mackenzie and McTavish, Frobisher & Company. No conclusive explanation is to be found in any contemporary correspondence or other record that has survived. Even Roderick fails to provide a reason, his only comment being the cryptic one that neither Mackenzie nor McTavish, Frobisher felt inclined to discuss a new contract "owing to an unfortunate misunderstanding between Mr. Mackenzie and Mr. McGillivray so that they cannot act well together." As for the cousins' long habit of correspondence, this lapsed for some years and reveals nothing except that on Mackenzie's side relations became positively frosty. After an unsuccessful attempt to detach his kinsman from service with the Nor'Westers, the "Dear Roderic" and "Dear Rory" of earlier letters becomes "Dear Sir."

Much gossip and speculation attended the departure from the trade and from Canada of "Nor'West Mackenzie." One rumour was that Mackenzie wanted his name to appear in that of the firm. Alexander Henry the Elder, a long-time fur trader and merchant, noted in a letter to an old Detroit friend and business associate that

... the old N West Company is all in the Hands of McTavish, and McKensey [sic] is out; the latter went off in a pet, the cause as far as I can learn was who should be first — McTavish or McK. and as there could not be two Caesars in Rome one must remove.

A common view of the parting of the ways is that Mackenzie was the daring young agent who ran afoul of Simon McTavish, the conservative, senior member of the firm. Mackenzie, this theory goes, was the eager advocate of expanding trade via a cheap, Hudson Bay freight route and also reaching out for the China trade; McTavish resented any plan that would diminish the role of Montreal in the trade. However, Mackenzie was not the sole

Simon McTavish was but one of many Scotsmen in the fur trade. This was as true of the rank and file of the Hudson's Bay Company as it was of their several rivals in Montreal.

Why was there such a large percentage of Highland Scots working in the trade?

partner eager to exploit new markets. Until his sudden death in 1804, McTavish remained as expansion-minded as he was when he started out in the trade. He began to market furs in China by freighting them out of Boston on ships bought by the Company, an extremely unprofitable venture until, in the late 1790s, he agreed to cut costs to some extent by using John Jacob Astor as a shipping agent. And in 1800, McTavish would authorize the dispatch of William McGillivray's brother Duncan, and David Thompson, the Company's "astronomer and surveyor," to find a way through the Rocky Mountains to the Pacific.

McTavish's plans for expansion may well have included Mackenzie's two voyages.

A clue to this comes from the pen of that doughty, Aberdeen-born clergyman, John Strachan. Long before he acquired prominence as prelate and politician, Strachan managed to keep up with much that was going on in the slowly developing provinces of Upper and Lower Canada. This included, of course, various doings of note in the fur trade, far and away the most important single industry in British North America. While relaying local news to an old friend in Scotland, Strachan suddenly remarks,

You have no doubt seen McKinsie's [Mackenzie's] voyage across the continent, which settles the long disputed North West Passage in the negative. He is a man of great intrepidity and considerable presence of mind. But the praise he acquired, tho' not diminished, should be extended to some of his Mercantile associates, particularly to a Mr. McTavish, the first merchant in the two provinces, were it generally known that he was the original projector, and pushed it [exploration] forward.

Another clue that credits McTavish was recorded by yet another Scot — Thomas Douglas, fifth Earl of Selkirk, who visited Upper and Lower Canada in 1803/04. In the course of a brief stay in Montreal, Lord Selkirk met and chatted with "most of the grandees, nabobs, of the N. W. Co.," and several of their trade colleagues, one of whom was Isaac Todd. Todd, a veteran Montreal fur merchant, remarked to Selkirk that Alexander Mackenzie was guilty of "unfair private conduct towards them [Nor'Wester management] as well as misrepresentations, in his book - he has certainly been unfair in not stating that it was McT. [McTavish] who planned both his expeditions. . . ."

Now, Todd's remarks may have been nothing more

than table talk of a somewhat biased nature. After all, he
and McTavish were friends of long standing. Yet there
are several intriguing pieces of circumstantial evidence
that suggest that what Strachan told Brown and what
Todd said to Selkirk may well have been true.

The manuscript of the 1789 expedition, preserved
today in the British Museum, is entitled "Journal of a
Voyage performed by Order of the N. W. Company, in a
Bark Canoe in search of a Passage by Water through the
N. W. Continent of America from Athabasca to the
Pacific Ocean in Summer 1789." In the *Voyages from
Montreal*, there is no mention of "by Order of the N. W.
Company." The title is simply "Journal of a Voyage, etc."

Second, several of Mackenzie's biographers say or
imply that, initially, he kept his intention to explore
northward in 1789 secret from everyone except Roderick.
Yet a letter Mackenzie sent to Grand Portage to the agents
of the North West Company 12 days before he set off on
his first voyage certainly implies that McTavish, Frobisher knew that he was going off exploring. Mackenzie
himself comes close to admitting that his explorations
were a continuance of the Company's expansionist policy.
On the first page of the Preface to the *Voyages* he
remarks on

... the practicability of penetrating across the continent of
America .... The general utility of such a discovery has been
universally acknowledged; while the wishes of my particular
friends and commercial associates that I should proceed in the
pursuit of it, contributed to quicken the execution of this favourite
project of my own ambition.

Furthermore, Mackenzie spent the winter of 1791/92
(the year immediately preceding the dash to the Pacific)
in London, England, mastering the techniques of sur-
veying. He sailed for Montreal in May 1792, reached
Fort Chipewyan in October and, in November, the site
of Fort Fork on the Peace River, *where men had been
busy since the spring of '72 felling and trimming timber
with which to build a wintering post.* Doesn't it seem
logical that Mackenzie was given leave of absence to
improve his navigational skills and that, in his absence,
management made arrangements whereby he could
employ these skills as soon as possible after he returned
to Athabasca?

It will be remembered that Mackenzie fails to

acknowledge his geographical debt to Peter Pond. And in the *Voyages*, Mackenzie would have us believe that he set off on the exploration of 1789 to settle "the dubious point of a practicable North-West passage" and that his second exploration determined "the practicability of a commercial communication through the continent of North America." Each of these statements is something less than truthful. Is it, then, very surprising that he would omit to mention executive initiation, approval, and encouragement of his explorations?

There is a strong possibility that the rift between Alexander Mackenzie and Simon McTavish was not as simple as youth versus age or, as has been suggested, because of disagreement over corporate policy. It is true that Mackenzie disliked the Company's expensive connection with Astor. Letters Mackenzie wrote during the three months he spent in New York City in 1798 reveal that he was extremely concerned about the costs of using American ports and shipping facilities. And it is also true that Mackenzie was convinced the future of the trade lay in a transport route through Hudson Bay, not via Montreal. Despite all this, a more likely explanation for the break between the two men is the thrust of Mackenzie's ambition to get to the top, where he could make major decisions and implement them. There are hints of this in McGillivray's correspondence, none of which prove anything; but they suggest that Mackenzie was impatient with his junior-partner status in a firm in which his fellow agent, William McGillivray, was being groomed for executive office.

If Mackenzie failed to realize his ambitions under the auspices of McTavish, Frobisher, within two years he achieved a very different kind of success. In mid-December 1801, the *Voyages from Montreal* was published simultaneously in London and Edinburgh, a large, quarto volume of 550 pages illustrated by maps and containing an engraving of the author from the portrait by Sir Thomas Lawrence. The book became a bestseller. Aided by generally favourable reviews and made popular by serialization in magazines, within two years of publication it had reappeared in several editions, including three in the United States, and in three other languages. At a time when the conduct of Britain's war with Napoleon Bonaparte was uninspired and unsuccessful

Alexander Mackenzie's great friend, William McGillivray, was a lanky, good-looking, Highland Scot with hair as flamingly orange-red as his clan's tartan. Like Mackenzie, McGillivray was a nine-year veteran of active fur trading in the pays d'en-haut. In time, he became the chief executive of the North West Company and for years managed its affairs very successfully and not a little ruthlessly. However, another Scot ultimately ruined the North West Company — and McGillivray with it.

Who was this man? How did he defeat McGillivray?

and the British badly needed a hero, Alexander Mackenzie supplied a focus for hero-worship. Within fourteen months of the book's appearance, he had been knighted by King George III and quickly became the favourite guest of every notable London hostess. On a visit to Scotland to see his two sisters, a great ball was organized for him in the town of Ayr.

When the author of the *Voyages* remarks in the Preface that he "is not a candidate for literary fame," there is a deeper significance to his statement than the honest admission that his style of writing lacked distinction. He was offering the general reader a travel book in the form of an explorer's logbook — but he was also offering readers in high places an economic treatise on the fur trade, and policies for a mighty expansion of it under the British flag. Mackenzie presents himself in the Preface as the hard-bitten, tough-minded fur trader who not only contemplated the "practicability of penetrating across the continent of America" but was "animated by the desire to undertake the perilous enterprise." However, he was addressing a totally different audience when he crisply observed in the same Preface that

Some account of the fur trade of Canada . . . of the native inhabitants, and of the extensive districts connected with it [the Northwest], forms a preliminary discourse, which will, I trust, prove interesting to a nation whose general policy is blended with, and whose prosperity is supported by the pursuits of commerce.

This "preliminary discourse," entitled "A General History of the Fur Trade from Canada to the North-West," occupies approximately *one quarter* of the entire book.

The essence of Mackenzie's reasoning is in the very last paragraphs of the *Voyages*, a clever, plausible argument but also a strangely prophetic vision of a British North America extending from sea to sea:

. . . the Columbia* [River] is the line of communication from the Pacific Ocean . . . its banks . . . suitable to the residence of a civilized people . . . By opening up this intercourse between the Atlantic and Pacific Oceans and forming regular establishments through the interior and at both extremes as well as along the coasts and islands, the entire command of the fur trade of North America might be obtained . . . except that portion of it which the Russians have in the Pacific. To this may be added the fishing in both seas, and the markets of the four quarters of the globe. Such would be the field for commercial enterprise, and incalculable would be the produce of it, when supported by the operations of

*The route of the Columbia River was not generally known at this time. Mackenzie was mistakenly talking of the river he had been on — the Fraser — which he thought entered the Pacific at the Columbia's mouth (46°20'N, 124°W), which was discovered in 1792 by Captain Robert Gray of the American merchantman Columbia. But Mackenzie's intuition was right: the Columbia was the navigable water route between the Rocky Mountains and the Pacific, as David Thompson would prove in 1811/12.

that credit and capital which Great Britain so pre-eminently possesses.

As a Canadian historian has remarked, "The port of Vancouver and the Province of British Columbia are an answer to that prophecy."

WORLD TRADE IN FURS: PRINCIPAL EXPORT ROUTES, 1783-1840

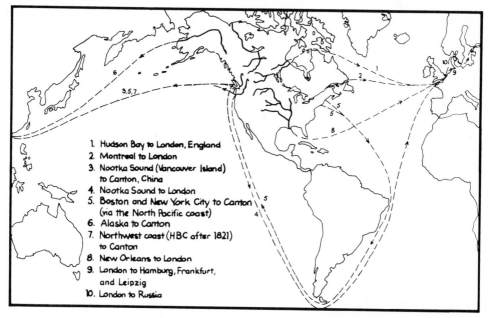

1. Hudson Bay to London, England
2. Montreal to London
3. Nootka Sound (Vancouver Island) to Canton, China
4. Nootka Sound to London
5. Boston and New York City to Canton (via the North Pacific coast)
6. Alaska to Canton
7. Northwest coast (HBC after 1821) to Canton
8. New Orleans to London
9. London to Hamburg, Frankfurt, and Leipzig
10. London to Russia

Mackenzie was not content to enlist the sympathy of the general reader, who enjoyed an adventure story that reflected the hard-driving nature of its author and ignored his economic pleas. In January 1802, barely a month after the publication of the *Voyages,* he submitted a detailed plan of imperial and commercial expansion to Lord Hobart, Secretary of State for War and the Colonies. Entitled "Preliminaries to the Establishment of a Permanent British Fishery and Trade in Furs &c. on the Continent and West Coast of North America," it is Mackenzie at his shrewdest and his most persuasive. The scope both of his thinking and his ambition is bold. Mackenzie was proposing nothing less than the occupation of part of the North Pacific coast by the British government and a linkage of that coast with the St. Lawrence via a unified, regulated fur trade. His plan neatly conjoined imperial interest and private enterprise, which could hardly be expected to prosper without something of the special privileges given the Hudson's Bay, East India, and South Sea Companies. Mackenzie's solution was to establish yet another chartered company — a London-based "Fishery and Fur Company" — under the legal protection of the British government. And since at this time the western-most portion of the international boundary ran only as far as the Rocky Mountains, he was, in effect, nudging the British government to stake a claim to what are now the states of Washington and Oregon — if not also the states of Montana and Idaho.

Lord Hobart suggested that the first step was to organize the union of all the Montreal fur interests, rather than just that of the old and new North West Companies, and Mackenzie left for Montreal in March 1802 to attempt this. By proposing this initial move, Lord Hobart was able to gloss over an awkward fact. The British government was not anxious to interfere with the vested rights of the Hudson's Bay, East India, and South Sea Companies and did not have men and ships to spare to establish and maintain garrisons halfway round the world in the Pacific Northwest.

In October 1802, Mackenzie wrote from Montreal to Lord Hobart to report that he had not succeeded in bringing about a merger of fur interests. He had returned to find the trade plagued once more by the old evils of competition. Nor'Westers and XY men were at each others' throats — sometimes quite literally — and Mackenzie's time and energy had to be spent, as during his first years in the interior, in fighting for a share of the trade.

Although he had left Montreal in the fall of 1799, Mackenzie had promptly returned in the spring of 1800 to take part in the creation of a stronger XY Company by the inclusion of yet another fur company, Parker, Gerrard & Ogilvy, which had also begun to contest the Nor'-Westers. In 1801, this association of interests became known as Alexander Mackenzie & Company, and in 1802 as Sir Alexander Mackenzie & Company although the more common reference to it was as the XY Company.*

Even with Mackenzie's experienced advice, the contest was hardly waged on equal terms. Each organization was

*The reason the Nor'Westers almost always referred to the opposition as the XY Company seems to be that, from the start, the bales, kegs, and pièces of the Company bore the brand XY, just as those of the older company bore the shipping label NW.

spending roughly similar amounts of money on goods and services, but the Nor'Westers had a decided edge in capital and in experienced personnel. However, the worst feature of the struggle was the extent to which each company lavished bribes of liquor on its customers. Exploitation and corruption of Indians was conducted on a scale never seen before. At the height of the struggle, the XY Company was using an average of 5,000 gallons of spirits a year. But the Nor'Westers, with the advantage of freight boats on the Great Lakes as well as canoe brigades, were employing at least 15,000 gallons annually in their trading operations. Liquor flowed like water in the pays d'en haut, and traders' journals casually record many commonplace incidents of mayhem and murder.

Debauching the western tribes as a matter of basic policy was at its worst between 1802 and 1804 and might have gone on for several years had it not been for the sudden illness and death of Simon McTavish early in July 1804. With the "old lion of Montreal" gone, the cooler wisdom of his successor, McGillivray, prevailed.

At the partners' summer meeting at Grand Portage in 1803, McGillivray noted that while the latest gross profits were the largest in the Company's history, five costly years of opposition had steadily reduced net returns and necessitated the introduction of still further economies. In addition, there had been rumours of "regulations of control" of the trade by British officials angered by accounts of drunken, demoralized Indians. Thus, after the news of his uncle's death reached him at Fort William late in July 1804, McGillivray was back in Montreal the next month. By October, he had negotiated terms of union with Sir Alexander Mackenzie & Company "to put an end to opposition and to avoid the waste of property attending thereon and to carry on the trade in a more advantageous manner...." McGillivray's opponents, too, were worried enough by years of expensive competition and the thought of government control to welcome a coalition.

From Mackenzie's point of view, it was 1787 all over again, when Gregory, McLeod had merged with the North West Company. If you can't beat your enemies, join them. However, although Mackenzie was allowed back into Nor'Wester ranks as a partner, his defection had not been forgotten, and was not going to be forgiven.

The amalgamation proved to be another setback in

The significance of 20,000 gallons of spirits being handed out in the period 1802-04 is that, in the years immediately prior to 1802, the North West Company averaged about 9,000 gallons annually.

In 1802/03, Nor'Wester profits were just short of £200,000.

Mackenzie's career. In 1802, he had been unsuccessful in imposing the logic of his views upon the British government or the rival companies. In 1804, he was effectively shut out of the Montreal fur trade. The further reorganization of the North West Company in November of that year expanded the number of shares to 100, but the division of them was on a three-to-one basis: 75 to the Nor'Westers and 25 to their former rivals. Control remained in the hands of McTavish, Frobisher, and Mackenzie was denied any hand in management.

After the amalgamation, the North West Company under McGillivray's leadership went on to compete with a more active Hudson's Bay Company and to expand the fur trade. Simon Fraser followed Mackenzie's old route up the Peace and Parsnip Rivers into what is now central British Columbia and established the Company's New Caledonia Department. David Thompson, Fraser's friend and fellow wintering partner, found two passes through the Rocky Mountains and built up the Columbia Department. Ultimately, in 1811/12, Thompson found the navigable canoe route to and from the Pacific that Mackenzie (and Fraser) had failed to find — the Columbia River. Its discovery was to give the Company a further ten years of life.

All of these activities and successes must have brought Mackenzie both pleasure and pain. His explorations had been fully justified, yet he had had absolutely no hand in directing their fulfilment. The only role his former Nor'Wester associates allowed Mackenzie was that of their representative in England. He lobbied support for the Company in government and royal circles. For example, in 1808 Mackenzie attempted to secure a trade charter from the British government that would give the Nor'Westers the same rights on the Pacific that the Hudson's Bay Company enjoyed in the interior of the continent. His arguments were impressive. In 1803, the United States had bought France's remaining holdings in North America, and the Louisiana Purchase as it was called had added to the States a vast region stretching from the Mississippi to the Rocky Mountains. Two years later, President Thomas Jefferson had sent the Lewis and Clark expedition to stake an early American claim to sovereignty of the Pacific Coast. Thus the lands and trade of the Columbia Basin could fall into American hands.

The official crest of the North West Company. (Note that, as with the Beaver Club, the key word is "Perseverance.")

The Nor'Westers' great rival, the Hudson's Bay Company, is still in business. The North West Company is not. What happened to the organization?

Nothing ever came of Mackenzie's proposal.

Because he had good reason to distrust the slow progress of government towards a point of ultimate action, in 1808 Mackenzie began to buy Hudson's Bay Company stock, which had sunk from £100 to £60 a share, thanks to the aggressive trading practices of the Nor'Westers. His object was to purchase control of the Company's operations and secure at least Hudson Bay transit rights for the Nor'Westers, if not also exclusive trading rights in Athabasca. Ironically, Mackenzie was aided this time by the wealthier Lord Selkirk, who had his own reasons for seeking power to manage HBC policy. By 1810, Mackenzie, Selkirk, and a group of associates had invested several thousand pounds in HBC stock. But by this time the former had discovered his ally's motive — the establishment of a settlement in the Nor'Westers' Red River Department — and Mackenzie opposed Selkirk's plan. Mackenzie sensed trouble: if farming spread all over a region where buffalo, the source of huge Nor'Wester supplies of pemmican, were accustomed to roam freely, the great herds would abandon the Red River region. This could create immense difficulties, if not hardship, for men serving in the pays d'en haut.

By February 1811, Selkirk had not only persuaded the Governor and Committee of the Hudson's Bay Company to accept his colonization scheme but had gained total personal control of it. Thereupon, Mackenzie, as a shareholder, sought to delay matters by insisting — as he had a right to — that Selkirk's project be examined and approved by a General Court of the Company, that is, by a general meeting of all shareholders. This manoeuvre also gave Mackenzie a breathing space in which to try to purchase enough further shares to sway a decision against Selkirk at the General Court. But few shares became available, and time ran out on Mackenzie. In the course of the general meeting, Selkirk was able to persuade the shareholders to accept the colonization venture. On that last day of May 1811, the Red River colony was born.

In the years following 1812, Sir Alexander's involvement in fur-trade matters was little more than that of a consultant. He was still a partner in the North West Company, and Edward ("Bear") Ellice, a fellow partner and London businessman, often sought his comments and advice on the gradual revival of competition and violence

The two men Mackenzie could neither walk over nor win over were Simon McTavish and Lord Selkirk.

What was it that made Selkirk such a stubborn opponent of Mackenzie and every last one of his Nor'-Wester colleagues?

in the pays d'en haut. The Nor'Westers were now battling
an aroused Selkirk and his followers and also traders
from the Bay, who were moving well inland and even
setting up shop in the Athabasca country. But with
William McGillivray now travelling to London to transact
Company business and even submitting his proposals to
the government for expansion, there was less and less for
Mackenzie to do. In any case, he had had his fill of knock-
ing on official doors and getting nowhere. In May, 1811,
he helped draw up a petition, addressed to King George
III, requesting that, in particular, the North West Company be given exclusive trading privileges between the
Rocky Mountains and the Pacific. But the request was
disallowed. A similar appeal in June 1812 to a government trade committee was unsuccessful. And yet another
petition in 1812, this time addressed to a cabinet minister,
was refused.

Lord Selkirk's interest was, in his own words, "at the western extremity of Can-ada, upon the Waters which fall into Lake Winnipeck [sic]," where, "with a moder-ate exertion of industry" colonists could be sure of a "comfortable subsistence." He dreamed of founding a settlement — and did.

Early in 1819, Mackenzie renewed correspondence
with Roderick (now addressed as "My Dear Sir"), after
allowing contact to lapse for almost two years. In the
letter he mentions learning about Selkirk's struggle with
the Nor'Westers from the newspapers, and goes on to
remark with great shrewdness that he would not be
surprised to see a serious change take place in the direction of the North West Company's affairs. He adds,

. . . I have been overtaken with the consequences of my sufferings
in the North West. I think it is of the same nature with Mr.
McGillivray's complaint, but it has not yet arrived at a serious
crisis. I have, in obedience to orders, become a water drinker and
milk sop. I have not tasted wine, spirituous or malt liquor for
several months, which I think has been of service to me.
   The symptoms of the disorder are very disagreeable and most
uncomfortable. The exercise of walking, particularly if uphill,
brings on a headache, stupor or dead pain, which at once pervades
the whole frame, attended with a listlessness and apathy which I
cannot well describe.
   Yours truly and sincerely,

                              Alex. Mackenzie

Now 55, he had just about a year to live. His "disorder" seems to have been Bright's disease, a term applied
to various forms of bacterial infection, and gradual
degeneration, of the kidneys. It was probably caused by
the primitive conditions he had endured for so many
years in the pays d'en haut. (In the course of returning

from the Pacific he casually noted a swelling of the ankles that made walking very difficult and very painful; this is one symptom of Bright's disease.) Dieting and rest prolonged his life into 1820, but in May of that year Roderick received a letter from a Mr. Kenneth Dowie.

Dear Sir,

It is with the greatest regret I have to inform you of the death of my uncle Sir Alexander Mackenzie.

Accompanied by Lady Mackenzie and children, he was on his way from Edinburgh to [Avoch] Rosshire and was suddenly taken ill at Mulnain, near Dunkeld, on the 11th of March and expired the following morning.

Epilogue

Barely 12 months after Alexander Mackenzie's body was laid to rest, the British government was induced, principally by the lobbying of Montreal and London fur merchants, to arrange a merger of the North West Company and the Hudson's Bay Company under the name of the latter, and grant it a monopoly of trade throughout the entire western interior and on the Pacific coast. This union, formally signed on March 27, 1821, vindicated the logic of Mackenzie's commercial view. Unable to overcome the Hudson's Bay Company's great advantage of cheaper, direct access to the pays d'en haut and thus to the Pacific, the Nor'Westers were forced by years of steadily rising costs to accept terms of union with the Bay organization.

As for Mackenzie's political reasons for a unified, expanded fur trade, this new, stronger Hudson's Bay Company, under the leadership of another Highland Scot, George Simpson, went on to challenge the Russians and the Americans on the Pacific coast and succeeded in establishing a British claim to a large part of the continental Northwest. This claim had far-reaching results. In 1846, when the British and American governments negotiated a settlement of the boundary beyond the Rocky Mountains, the United States secured what was known as the Oregon Territory, but Great Britain retained those regions immediately north of the 49th parallel that later became known as British Columbia. Without an outlet on the Pacific, it is extremely doubtful if there would ever have been a Canada.

Further Reading

Every biography of Alexander Mackenzie concentrates on little else but his explorations. And all his biographers have idolized him. To each and every one of them, he was Superman: daring, dauntless, and unblemished by normal human faults and failings. The same is true of those who have produced the various editions of the *Voyages from Montreal* — with one marvellous exception. The Introduction to W. Kaye Lamb's edition of *The Journals and Letters of Sir Alexander Mackenzie* (Macmillan, 1971) contains an excellent account of his character, life, and work. This book also includes every known letter or part of a letter written by Mackenzie (except business correspondence on strictly corporate matters). These vary considerably in importance and interest because most of his personal papers were lost when his home, Avoch House, was destroyed by fire thirteen years after his death.

A great deal of romantic nonsense has been written about the fur trade, but there are some very dependable books on the subject. A few are listed below.

The Course of Empire, B. DeVoto, Boston: Houghton, Mifflin, 1952.
David Thompson, James K. Smith. Toronto: Fitzhenry & Whiteside, 1975.
The Explorers of North America, 1492-1806, T. B. Brebner. New York: Doubleday, 1955.
The Fur Trade, Rosemary Neering. Toronto: Fitzhenry & Whiteside, 1974.
Fur Trade Canoe Routes of Canada/Then and Now, E. W. Morse. Ottawa: Queen's Printer, 1969.
Growth of a Nation Study Print Program. Toronto: Fitzhenry & Whiteside, 1973.
Montreal and the Fur Trade, E. E. Rich. Montreal: McGill University Press, 1966.
The North West Company, M. W. Campbell. Toronto: Macmillan, 1973.
The Pedlars from Quebec, and Other Papers on the Nor'Westers, W. S. Wallace. Toronto: The Ryerson Press, 1954.

Editing Laura Damania
Design: Jack Steiner
Cover Illustration: Merle Smith

The Canadians

Consulting Editor: Roderick Stewart
Editor-in-Chief: Robert Read